CRADLE OF CULTURE

CRADLE

1800-1810 THE

by Reese Davis James

OF CULTURE

PHILADELPHIA STAGE

Author of *Old Drury of Philadelphia*

Philadelphia   UNIVERSITY OF PENNSYLVANIA PRESS

© 1957 BY THE TRUSTEES OF THE
UNIVERSITY OF PENNSYLVANIA

PUBLISHED IN GREAT BRITAIN, INDIA, AND PAKISTAN
BY THE OXFORD UNIVERSITY PRESS
LONDON, BOMBAY, AND KARACHI

LIBRARY OF CONGRESS CATALOGUE CARD NO.: 56-12703

MANUFACTURED IN THE UNITED STATES OF AMERICA BY
BOOK CRAFTSMEN ASSOCIATES, INC., NEW YORK

TO GRACE

but for whose watchfulness
this book had never been

Prologue

This is a book about the Chestnut Street Theatre, erected on the North side of Chestnut Street, Philadelphia, just above Sixth, ten years after the end of the Revolution and five years after the lifting of the ban on the playhouses.

It is a book about its actors and actresses, some of whom were of England's best and among the first of their profession to brave the hazards of an Atlantic crossing and the hardships of the New World.

It is a book about their roles, their songs, their recitations.

It is a book about the Chestnut's dancers, who did so much to beguile a people still at grips with a wilderness and the task of building a democracy.

It is a book about the Chestnut's scenic artists, who created the Gothic Halls and Fairy Grottoes for its melodramas, ballets and pantomimes.

It is a book about its managers, Wignell and Reinagle, then Warren and Wood, and their enterprise in establishing it as the finest in America of its time.

It is a book about the growth of a city and a country and the role the Chestnut played, as a "cradle of culture," in awakening national spirit and appreciation of the fine arts in the critical period immediately after the death of Washington.

Contents

	Page
PROLOGUE	7
1. The Theatre Loses a Patron, 1799-1800	15
2. Circus and Spectacle, 1800-1801	25
3. Whirligig and Witchcraft, 1801-1802	36
4. A Great Manager Passes, 1802-1803	47
5. First Jefferson and First Melodrama, 1803-1804	57
6. History Takes a Bow, 1804-1805	66
7. Enter the Censor, 1805-1806	75
8. Patriotism and Pantomime, 1806-1807	86
9. Audience Reaction: The Embargo, 1807-1808	96
10. Panoply, 1808-1809	106
11. Warren Wood, 1809-1810	113
Epilogue	121
Appendix A. List of Plays, Ballets, Pantomimes, and Musical Entertainments	127
Appendix B. List of Performers	140
Index	143

Illustrations

(The illustrations appear as a group following page 64)

The "Cradle of Culture"
Thomas Cooper
John Hodgkinson
William Warren
Thomas Wignell
Joseph Jefferson
James Fennell
Mrs. William Wood
Mrs. William Francis
Alexander Reinagle
John Howard Payne
William Wood
Mrs. William Warren
William Francis

CRADLE OF CULTURE

1

The Theatre Loses a Patron
1799-1800

ONLY TWO WEEKS after the opening of its season on December 4, 1799, the Chestnut Street Theatre closed its doors out of respect for the memory of a great American who had done so much to counteract the effect of Quaker prejudice against the stage. Upon receiving the unhappy news of Washington's death at Mount Vernon on December 14, the managers draped the theatre in black and prepared, for December 23, an appropriate bill of music and drama. The curtain was slowly lifted on an affecting scene of a tomb, in the center of which was a portrait of the sage and hero, encircled by oak leaves. On the pyramidal top of the "catafalque" perched an eagle weeping tears of blood. The company, assembled on the stage and somberly clad (among them the sprightly Elizabeth Arnold, later the mother of Edgar Allan Poe), sang occasional music by Reinagle, Austrian by birth but one of America's first composers. Wignell, co-manager with Reinagle, delivered a monody on the death of Washington, whom he had often lighted to his box; and Warren, later to marry Wignell's widow, played Horatius in *The Roman Father,* a tragedy Washington liked for its appeal to the liberty-loving.

Some of the ladies in the audience, wearing black badges for the occasion, could remember Washington at one of his Presidential levees when he bowed to his guests, clad in purple satin or black velvet, his hair in full dress, powdered and gathered behind in a large silk bag. They could recall his yellow gloves and cocked hat, its edges adorned with a black feather about an inch deep [sic], his knee and shoe buckles and long sword with its finely wrought and polished steel hilt and its scabbard of polished white leather. Some of the gentlemen present could remember Washington (as they doubtless preferred), cantering with his officers, "All dressed," as the playwright Dunlap describes them, "in the old staff uniform of the United States, blue and buff, with the black and white cockade, marking the union with France, in their cocked hats, which were worn, as generally at that time in the American army, with the greatest breadth (to use a sea phrase), fore and aft, so as to screen the eyes." Perhaps a few of the men in the audience had seen the "gallantly equipped and mounted" cavalcade, their gold epaulets glittering in the sun and, like Dunlap, a goggle-eyed youth of seventeen at the time, had doffed their cocked hats to the tall figure in the center, who, with his staff, had returned the salute with waving plumes.

Washington's death cast a shadow over the opening theatrical season of the new century but it quickened the patriotism his victories had evoked. The bills at the Chestnut were both a response and an appeal to public sentiment. On December 30, the day of a funeral procession in the General's honor and a eulogium by Henry Lee to the hero who (as he said) was "first in war, first in peace and first in the hearts

The Theatre Loses a Patron

of his countrymen," the Chestnut's managers repeated the monody and, with Dunlap's *The Stranger,* offered a dramatic sketch "interspersed with song, dance and spectacle," entitled *The Constellation or a Wreath for American Tars,* extolling an infant Navy's challenge to the victories of Princeton, Trenton, and Yorktown. The Chestnut's scenic artists, Milbourne and Holland, who had been imported from England, combined their ingenuity to reconstruct the action between Old Ironsides' sister ship and the ship *L'Insurgente,* which had capitulated in the Caribbean the previous February 9. As much in the Elizabethan tradition of teaching history from the stage as in answer to popular demand, Wignell and Reinagle, on April 8, produced a dramatic sketch entitled *A Wreath for American Tars or Huzza Again for the Constitution,* in which their artists simulated her engagement with *La Vengeance,* a prize of which Truxton, famed privateer, was cheated through the damage his ship had sustained. Washington was mourned in an "elegiac ode," on April 22, accompanied by "vocal and instrumental music dedicated to the memory of the late illustrious Chief of the Armies of the United States" and, two nights later, after a musical entertainment entitled *The Naval Pillar,* there was a display of emblematic transparent scenery, popular for a number of years to come, with an "apotheosis of the late illustrious Lt. General Washington designed by Mr. Holland and executed by Mr. Milbourne, Mr. Holland, Mr. Robins and Mr. Stewart."

This was a tribute to a patron of the theatre as well as to a nation's leader. Washington had graced the Southwark with his presence just a year after the ban on the playhouses had been lifted. With the opening of its successful rival, the Chestnut, the General welcomed the opportunity of escaping the cares of office in attending performances of *The School for Scandal, The Poor Soldier,* and others of his favorite pieces, despite a lingering prejudice against the acting of plays that threatened the success of the new venture.

Its start in 1793 had been far from auspicious. Yellow fever, imported from San Domingo, had deferred the opening of the Chestnut and taxed the resources of Wignell and Reinagle, who were compelled to house and clothe a company of fifty-six performers while the plague abated. The theatre, with its interior modeled after the theatre at Bath, was sumptuous as compared with the barn-like structure at South and Apollo streets, resembling it only in the identical motto over its stage, "The Eagle Suffers Little Birds to Sing," the Southwark's way of alluding to the recent ban. In the Chestnut's accommodations for 1155 persons a sacrifice had been made in the interest of art. It was smaller than the Park of New York, much smaller than Drury Lane or Covent Garden; but its excellent acoustics relieved its players of having to indulge in the exaggerated gesturing and rant so common abroad. From its opening on February 17, 1794, to the start of the new century, its company had established a reputation as America's best, with 225 new pieces, among them Shakespeare's *As You Like It* and *Coriolanus,* Beaumont and Fletcher's *Rule a Wife and Have a Wife,* farces by O'Keeffe, comedies by Mrs. Cowley, Mrs. Inchbald, and the younger Colman, and tragedies by Cumberland. Meanwhile, Wignell had won a place in Washington's affection; and Mrs. Merry, at sixteen acclaimed in London as "another Siddons" and now the Chestnut's Juliet and Ophelia, ate venison and turtle and drank madeira with the city's elite and drove to their homes in a "chariot of simple but elegant construction, drawn by two very favored sorrell horses, well matched and of great beauty and docility."

It is inevitable that some of Mrs. Merry's experiences in the theatre were to be rather less pleasant. The city was pushing its boundaries beyond Callowhill and Cedar streets on the North and South and the rivers on the East and West;

The Theatre Loses a Patron

and, while its 70,000 was meagre as compared with its present population, it exceeded New York's by 10,000. Washington's presence in the Southwark, and later the Chestnut, had been enough to hold in check the grog-drinking gallery gods, whose insulting remarks were occasionally pointed at the boxes. As he presided austerely at the pianoforte Reinagle could exert a quieting influence and Wignell could anticipate disturbances by requesting ladies and gentlemen to dispatch their servants to retain their places in the boxes before curtain time "at candle light."

But out of the vigorous politics of the period arose contingencies for which the managers were unable to provide. On January 1, John Randolph had alluded in Congress to the national troops as "mercenaries and ragamuffins"; and, while he was visiting the theatre that night to witness the spectacle of *Blue Beard,* he became the butt of abuse by army officers sitting near him. Upon viewing a procession upon the stage, one of them remarked to the other, "These are well-looking mercenaries." When Randolph ignored the reference, they came into his box and stood behind him. One of them said, regarding the actors in the pageant, "They are black Virginia ragamuffins." In the account of an eyewitness, "One of the officers, who was a very large man, then attempted to sit down alongside of Randolph and, the space being small, the latter was considerably bruised and hurt. Finally, the party left the box, one of them before he left pulling Randolph's cape." Randolph, instead of pleading Congressional immunity, embarrassed Adams by demanding a Presidential investigation. The incident fell just short of a "pistol appeal."

Indiscretion of any sort was dangerous in the early American playhouse. Five nights later a theatregoing gentleman was foolish enough to carry as much as $1,000 on his person and an opportunist cut it out of his pocket in true Elizabethan fashion. But in the wood-heated theatres of the time the danger of fire was a matter of sharper concern than political controversies or thefts, which are phenomena of every age. In handbills and advertisements Wignell pleaded with his patrons to refrain from smoking "segars," remembering that in 1798 the Boston Theatre was burnt and how, on the bitterly cold night that Philadelphia heard of Washington's death, the Chestnut was saved only by a contrary wind when Ricketts' Circus, across the street, like a funeral pyre to the dead hero, went up in flames that consumed the neighboring Oeller's Hotel, an event prophetic of the fires that destroyed the Richmond theatre eleven years later (at the cost of eleven lives, including the Governor's), the Chestnut itself after twenty years, and the Southwark theatre after twenty-one.

But in America's "new Athens" it would have taken more than a threat of fire to keep the Chestnut's patrons away from the theatre. Franklin's town was also the town of Carey, Parson Weems' publisher, of Charles Brockden Brown, inspirer of Poe, of Benjamin West, of Charles Willson Peale, museum founder, America's first taxidermist and painter of Revolutionary heroes (including Washington, of whom he did eight portraits), and the town of William Rush, carver of figureheads of ships in the harbor. Its citizens were eager to witness the ninety productions of the 1799-1800 season, including a half-dozen of Shakespeare's plays (*King John* for the first time in Philadelphia) and the works of more than twenty-six authors, including Sheridan's *The Critic*, Rowe's *The Fair Penitent*, and Otway's *Venice Preserved*. Among the ninety were twelve Philadelphia and seven American "firsts."

Patrons appreciated the efforts of an able company, particularly the comedy interpretations of Bernard, Portsmouth-born actor and friend of John Kemble. There was little to amuse them in Hopkins' Tony Lumpkin (his first appearance on any stage), though he was later to become the first husband of Elizabeth Arnold; but Cooper's return, on March 21, supplied the company with a much-needed and superlative Pierre (in *Venice Preserved*), King John, and Hamlet. The career of this actor had been meteoric. At nineteen a London success as Hamlet and Macbeth, he was now only twenty-four. His personality was arresting, both off and on the stage. Two years previously he had challenged a Philadelphia lawyer to a duel; and now, as he drove his tandem sulky, its entire seat and "silky body" covered by a "cloak, trimmed with gold lace," he carried a pair of dueling pistols in holsters on either side of the vehicle. A gun in a leathern case swung alongside. As he rode his "splendid charger" on highway or city street, "dressed in a blue coat, red waistcoat, buckskin breeches and fair-top boots," his reputation as a dead shot discouraged bandits or "ragamuffins" who might whistle at his finery. He could have routed them without a recourse to weapons. In the days before the iron horse he accomplished the feat of appearing in New York and Philadelphia on alternate nights by driving a gig at breakneck speed or by riding relays of horses, and he could walk the legs off most of the men in his audiences.

The managers' efforts were as unremitting as Cooper's on the road. In *Blue Beard,* advertised as having run 150 nights at Drury Lane, they produced an ocular feast with books of its popular songs on sale at the theatre or at Rice's bookstore on S. 2nd Street; in *Reconciliation,* on January 20, an American première of T. Dibdin's translation of Kotzebue's comedy and, in *The Castle Spectre,* a Philadelphia première, for which, on April 2, Milbourne and Holland prepared a "Gothic Hall," a "Grand Armoury, with piles of armour arranged as in the Tower of London," a "view of the River Conway," an "oratory of a Chapel," and a "distant view of Conway Castle by moonlight." On May 14, for *Pizarro,* Sheridan's adaptation of another Kotzebue piece, the painters created a "Magnificant Pavilion," a "Temple of the Sun," a "Wild Retreat among the Rocks."

Reinagle, as musical director, produced the original score for the opera of *The Double Disguise* and the musical accompaniments of thirteen comic operas, three dramas, and three farces. Songs he scheduled were Mrs. Marshall's as Little Pickle in *The Spoiled Child* on December 18; "Sweet Poll of Plymouth" by Darley in *The Positive Man* on March 12; George Stevens' "The Sea Storm" by a gentleman making his first appearance on any stage, also on March 12; "Giordanis" by Mrs. Oldmixon, on April 18; and a "song in character" by Hopkins in *Jacob Gawkey's Travels* on May 3. For the city of Joseph Hopkinson, who wrote the words of "Hail Columbia," and of the teacher who reputedly composed its music—a collaboration that frequently raised the curtain of the Chestnut and nearly spelled the doom of the actor Fox (too frequently treated in the taverns for singing it)—Reinagle also scheduled *The Catch Club,* which afforded a vehicle for the male voices of the theatre on May 2, Grétry's overture to *Richard Coeur de Lion* on January 13, and Reinagle's own "Masonic" overture to *Harlequin Freemason* on April 21.

Reinagle's task included the music for the ballets and incidental dances, admirably directed by the actor Francis, who joined in a "treble" hornpipe with Warrell, Jr., and Mitchell on March 12 and coached them, with Miss Solomon, for their "triple" hornpipe on April 18. The managers were properly gauging an already traditional love of music and the dance, further stimulated by emigrés from France and San Domingo. Outside the theatre the concerts of Miss Broadhurst and Mrs. Oldmixon were well attended, though Francis, one of the famed Assembly's early teachers, found the belles promenading the Philadelphia streets in their high-waisted, Greekish costumes and close-fitting hats as heavy-footed as they were nimble-witted, a terror to the beaux who

The Theatre Loses a Patron 23

ran the gamut of their vicious punning and saucy innuendoes.

Aware of a growing interest in better speech reflected in their repartee (a natural evolution of a people who could now turn to cultural pursuits) the managers included recitations in their bills: after *Henry IV, Part I,* "The Water Bottle or The Miraculous Cure," by Bernard on April 19; before *Harlequin Freemason,* on April 21, an occasional address in the character of Columbine by Mrs. Francis; and, after *The Suspicious Husband* on April 28, the poem of "Alonzo and Imogene," delivered by Cooper.

The oratory rolling from Congress Hall across the street may have played a part in whetting this taste for elocution, though what effect it was having, as far as Philadelphia was concerned, must presently come from reading the speeches as reported in the press. There were to be no more balls given in honor of President Adams at the Chestnut, where, on January 16, 1799, the "pit" had been "floored over" and dancing (foible of Washington) had continued "until 11 o'clock when a curtain drawing up discovered a splendid supper hall, decorated with new scenery and rendered significant by the motto over the President's box, 'Millions for defense but not one cent for tribute'," an allusion to Adams' vicarious answer to Tallyrand's blackmailing note of 1798. There were to be no more occasions such as Adams' visit to the Chestnut on December 30, 1799 or on February 26 of the following year, when *Gustavus Vasa, the Deliverer of His Country,* was given, just as it had been in honor of Washington. As if in farewell to Adams and the Congress, packing their belongings for the journey to the mosquito-infested swamps of Federal City, the managers staged a "grand display of emblematic transparent scenery," on April 24, with "the Apotheosis of the late illustrious Lt. General Washington, designed by Mr. Holland and executed by Mr. Milbourne, Mr. Holland, Mr. Robbins and Mr. Stuart."

The lawmakers, departing for the new capital of America, chosen for its neutral location and supposed immunity from yellow fever, were to miss their evenings at the Chestnut and, before long, to petition Wignell and Reinagle to open a "National Theatre" on the Potomac.

2

Circus and Spectacle
1800-1801

IN PIOUS ALLUSION to the fire that destroyed Ricketts' Circus, Elizabeth Drinker wrote in her *Journal,* on December 17, 1799, "If no person is hurt, or no poor horses burnt—no matter for the circus"; but she was giving vent to a Quaker prejudice at variance with the feeling of the average Philadelphian. The year it opened, 1793, Washington, lover of all things theatrical, attended a performance at Rickett's; and, in an era in which horses, except for rivers and canals, were the only means of transportation and the American public, still at grips with a wilderness, gloried in feats of endurance and physical skill, the circus was a form of entertainment which, except for the fire, might have supported the troupe across the street from the Chestnut for many years to come. Even Lailson's, an amphitheatre opening four years after Rickett's, could have survived the competition if its proprietor had been less extravagant in his ideas.

America's love of animals, particularly horses, drew Philadelphians to pony races and, in early May, to witness performances of Swan's dancing horse, which cavorted to the popular airs of "The President's March" and "Yankee Doodle." Lailson's had favored the town with Miss Vanice, first female equestrian to appear in the country; and Rickett's with the horsemanship of a young American named Hutchins, a "flying pyramid of five persons riding on three horses at one time", billed as never yet attempted, and with the astonishing maneuvers of Cornplanter, a horse that could "ungirth his saddle and take it off."

Lailson's great ninety-foot dome had collapsed and, now that Ricketts' lay in ashes, the town was eager for a renewal of circus performances. In order to supply them, together with dances, pantomimes, and plays, John Durang, gymnast, dancer, and actor, opened the South Street Theatre on May 1 with "The Thespian Panorama" over a fortnight before the Chestnut ended its season of 1799-1800.

Yellow Jack had departed. Since the erection of the Chestnut, it had taken more than eight thousand lives; but the tiny red flags over the doorways, betokening its presence, had vanished with the plague. Except for the weather Durang's only worry was the opposition of a group of amateur actors calling themselves the Thespian Society. It was "evident the intention of this strange gang, in assuming the title," ran a statement published by the Society, "is only to mislead the curious, and thereby gain a crowded house and consequently crowded pockets [for the Panorama]. The friends of the members are well assured that the object of the Thespian Society was not emolument. It is therefore hoped that the public will not countenance imposters."

Claiming priority to the title, Durang proceeded with an eleven-night season in which his activity was prodigious. In a mosquito-infested theatre, he danced on the slack wire on May 3 and tumbled on it on May 6. He tumbled on the slack

Circus and Spectacle 27

rope on June 2 and 7. On June 2 he also leaped through a barrel of fire (a pleasant avocation for a hot night) and, on June 7, executed a "variety of feats of activity" on Swan's horse. On June 7 Mrs. Rowson, one of several performers from the company burnt at Ricketts,' went "through the manual exercise." She repeated it on June 25 "in the character of an American volunteer" and, for that night only, Durang offered to "fly from the back part of the gallery upon the stage," to "dance on the wire," to "dance blindfold over a dozen of eggs," to "tumble on the slack rope," and, together with Rowson, his co-manager and members of his company, to assist "nine young men" of the city in a gymnastic stunt entitled "The Pyramids of Egypt."

Durang had promised to make the old theatre as comfortable as possible and the Southwark's bills were sufficiently interesting to keep the minds of its patrons off the heat and the locusts, which were having their year in Philadelphia. For music-lovers there were songs in *Rosina* on May 1, and "The Sailor Boy," with words by Mrs. Rowson, on June 7; "Hark, Hark from the Woodlands" and the "Little Sailor Boy" on June 9; "singing" on June 11; and a "favorite song" on June 25—all by Mrs. McDonald. There was also "A Twiggle and a Friz," with its singer unnamed, on June 11 as a finale to *Vintner in the Suds*. For disciples of Terpsichore there were dances in *Rosina*; a sailor's hornpipe by Durang on May 10, June 2, 9, and 16; "The Savage Dance," unexplained, on May 10; "Four and Twenty Fiddlers" by Durang on June 2; a hornpipe by Miss Popoote on June 9; and a hornpipe by a "young French lady" on June 16 and 25. On June 25, her benefit night, the roly-poly Mrs. Rowson displayed a questionable taste and shocked her admirers by dancing a hornpipe "in irons, bound hand and foot."

There were recitations, too. Durang spouted Shakespeare's "Seven Ages" on June 7 and, on June 16, Dr. Goldsmith's

"Epilogue" in the character of Harlequin, which he topped off with his flying leap through a barrel of fire. With the Rowsons to help him, Durang could produce for the first time in Philadelphia the pantomime of *Harlequin Mariner,* Farquhar's *The Recruiting Officer,* and the farce *Botheration.* The bustling season ended on July 5 when, appropriately for the date, he showed a transparency, first exhibited June 25 as the best likeness "ever taken" of Washington.

The humidity was as killing as ever. Philadelphians could console themselves with draughts of the icy well-water (killing draughts if downed too rapidly) or, with bound girls decamping to escape the sweltering weather, solve their servant problem and at the same time fortify themselves by consuming the delicious bluepoint oysters, terrapin, or celebrated pepper-pot dispensed at the Leopard Tavern.

But business at the Southwark must have been encouraging, for the actors Barrett and Hodgkinson, whilom pot-boy who had sung and fiddled his way to fame in the English and American theatres, opened the playhouse on July 30 for what amounted to a festival of song and recitation. After a six-year absence from Philadelphia he offered, on the opening night, some of Charles Dibdin's "new and popular songs not yet heard in America." Listed, as inferentially by the troubadour whom London flocked to hear in his little Leicester Square Theatre, were "The New Quack," "True Glory," "Country Club," "Now's the Time for Mirth and Glee," "Here's a Nice New Bow-Wow," "Frolicksome Fellow," and "Mounseer Nong-Tong-Paw." Hodgkinson repeated them on July 31; and, on August 4, he substituted for "The New Quack" and "Here's a Nice New Bow-Wow" the songs of "Negro Philosophy," "The Sailor's Journal", and "Professional Grinders." As for recitations, Barrett gave George Alexander Stevens' "Lecture on Heads" and Hodgkinson, it may be assumed, the Monody on Washington all

Circus and Spectacle

three nights. Hodgkinson delivered an "occasional address" on July 30.

At summer's end Prigmore, a buffoon who delighted the gallery but ruffled the boxes, attempted a five-night season at the Southwark. In what he termed a "theatric medley," he sang the song of "Nong-Tong-Paw," on August 23, and "The Hobbies" on August 23 and 25. He enlisted the services of Mrs. Durang and Mrs. Rowson for a double hornpipe on August 23, and of Durang on August 25 for performances on the slack wire and rope. He also had Mrs. Rowson to help him, on August 23 and 25, in the role of Sally Frolic in *The Touchstone of Truth,* and on the last night, September 10, a number of Philadelphia gentlemen, evidently of The Thespian Club (and as "amateurs," of course) in the principal parts of *The Mountaineers.* Prigmore gave a "humorous prologue" on August 25.

An anomaly of this impromptu season was what appeared to have been a national première on September 5 of an American "speaking piece" entitled *William Penn or the Landing of Our Forefathers.*

The Chestnut Street Company had meanwhile accepted an invitation to go to Washington where President Adams, involved in a stormy campaign resulting in the election of Jefferson, must have needed recreation. A large building, erected as a hotel and later the post- and patent-office, was available for theatrical performances. The hazards of the highway nine years prior to the first experimental railroad (a wood-railed, horsedrawn affair only forty-two yards long, precurser of the "land carriages") deferred the opening of the improvised playhouse when a storm of wind and rain destroyed the scenery carefully prepared in Philadelphia. But the audience finally assembled to greet them was surprisingly large for the size of the new capital and the players made theatrical history with Wignell, Cooper, and Mrs. Merry in the leading roles of *Venice Preserved.*

Having inaugurated this "national theatre," Wignell & Reinagle opened the Chestnut on October 6, 1800, with a benefit for yellow fever sufferers at Baltimore. This generosity proved an auspicious beginning for what proved to be a season in which the company, pronounced by *Dunlap,* the New York manager, as "rank [ing] higher" than his own, scored an artistic as well as a financial success. In 1800-1801 the managers could offer ninety-nine pieces, among them ten Philadelphia and six national premières including the American play of *Edwy and Elgiva,* never previously acted, although *Cato,* beloved of Washington and with a title role Washington had once expressed a wish to play, which was also billed as a Philadelphia first, had been offered in the town a half-century before. There were twenty tragedies, fourteen farces, twenty-six comedies, and fifteen comic operas included in the repertory, eight of them plays by Shakespeare.

Much of the entertainment was fresh from London. There were *The Law of Lombardy* and *The Siege of Belgrade* from Drury Lane; and, from Covent Garden, *St. David's Day,* new to America, *The Votary of Wealth,* and the English rustic comedy of *Speed the Plough,* celebrated for its ploughing match and for Dame Ashfield's oft-quoted question, "What will Mrs. Grundy say?" The managers failed with *Liberal Opinions,* new to America, but they showed initiative in securing a manuscript copy of the comedy from the patentee with a view to presenting it as speedily as possible.

They also strove to satisfy the current appetite for spectacle. While little larger than the "O" of Shakespeare's day, their stage of 71 feet in depth and 36 in width was ample enough for Milbourne and Holland to create a tolerable effect of a Turkish village, a blue magic chamber or a wood in which the "Spahis" were trapped in *Bluebeard,* on October 10, or a scene for an attack on Tilbury Fort, as after *The Critic* on October 20, or a "temple of the sun" or a "cavern and a dungeon," as in *Pizarro* on October 22. The staging of *The Siege of Oxydrace,* preceding the tragedy of *Alexander the Great,* on January 12 drew encomium from a dramatic critic, Oliver Oldschool (Joseph Dennie), man-about-town and theatre habitué, a familiar figure as he slipped along Chestnut Street in his pea-green coat, white vest, nankeen small clothes, and white silk stockings and pumps, fastened with silver buckles which covered at least half the foot from instep to toe. Years after he had grown to manhood, John's son, Charles Durang, stage historian, recalled the "splendor" with which *The Siege* was mounted.

The antique battering rams were in full operation. The scaling of the walls by Alexander and his officers was exciting. The warriors were poised on the large Grecian shields of the soldiery, who formed bridges, one rising above the other like turrets or platforms of scaffolding, forming a tortoise, as it was called in the bills. Over this shield work Alexander, Hephestian, etc., sword in hand, with their scaling ladders, mounted and threw the rope-ladders over the coping of the turrets. They climbed up, fighting at every step. They severally gained the top of the battlements and precipitated themselves, apparently into the city. On the bridge at the back [were] overwhelming numbers in hand to hand contention—receiving the darts of [their] enemies in a shield, plucking them out and hurling them back to the enemy. . . . They employed real horses in this piece, clad in full armorial housings, or coverings, a kind of scale armor [the pitiful salvage of the bankrupt Lailson's]. The battle and defeat of Porus we have never yet seen equalled in any of the present theatres [asserted Durang] with all their thrasonical bill-display and unmeasured puffing. The march into Babylon was a most imposing processional exhibition. The properties, banners and trophies, with eagles, elephants, lions, etc., were composed of papier-mache, in the most artistical style. The marchings of the troops in sections, hollow squares and phalanx, were most admirably performed by eighty marines from the Navy Yard, drilled by night rehearsals for the purpose.

corps needed little strengthening. The only other new player was a negligible actor named Usher, who bowed as Hassan in *The Castle Spectre* on November 3.

The dancing corps were well above average. On October 22 Master Harris and Miss Arnold appeared in a *minuet de la cour* and a "new gavote" and, on March 21 after *The Catch Club,* in a minuet. On December 1 and April 7, in Act II of *Speed the Plough,* there was a country dance by the characters after a ploughing match. On February 14 there was a "Spanish Fandango," composed by Francis and danced by Durang, Miss Arnold, and Miss Solomons. There was a "Caledonian Frolic" on March 9, a "Medley Hornpipe" by Francis and a new "straspey" by Durang, Francis, Miss Arnold, and Miss Solomons on March 14, and a triple hornpipe by Durang, Miss Arnold, and Miss Solomons on March 25.

The recitations were by the talented Bernard and Cooper. Bernard gave Michael Fortune's Prologue to *Management* on October 27; the Epilogue to *The East Indian* on December 19 and 24, in the character of the ghost of Queen Elizabeth; "The dissertation on Hobby Horses" on March 7; "Giles Gallop and Brown Sally Green" on February 9 and March 9; and the Epilogue to *Edwy and Elgiva* in the character [of the Fool?] on April 4. Cooper recited "Alonzo and Imogene" on February 18, March 9 and 23 (after *Venice Preserved*); Wignell did the Prologue to *Edwy and Elgiva* on April 4.

In the season ending April 11, 1801, the fanfare of Presidential visits had been missing from the Chestnut. With the nation's capital in Washington and a new and less colorful personality in the Executive Mansion, Philadelphia gave only passing notice to the death of Adams' son, Charles, as reported in the *Advertiser* of December 1, 1800. Writes Elizabeth Drinker:

Circus and Spectacle

Ye morning [of March 4, preceding the belated election of Jefferson on April 18, 1801,] was ushered in by the ringing of bells. There has been a great fuss in some parts of the city, [but] about us it was quiet, only that the guns from a vessel opposite Race Street fired 16 times, and being so near, were very loud. An ox was roasted whole, somewhere near the City, and there are many companies assembled at different Taverns.

But Philadelphians were more absorbed in local affairs. With the money raised by a benefit on February 18, the managers were bent on improving their theatre; and the cornerstone the city-fathers had laid, on October 18, 1800, for the Eastern abutment of the first permanent bridge over the Schuylkill, was a symbol of the hope they cherished for the expansion of Penn's greene countrie towne.

3

Whirligig and Witchcraft
1801-1802

TWO ILL-STARRED performers appeared in Philadelphia in the summer of 1801. They were Fullerton from the Theatre Royal, Liverpool, whom the Chestnut's managers had evidently chosen to fill the shoes of Cooper, temporarily lost to the Park in New York, and Robertson from Astley's Amphitheatre, London, extravagantly billed as the "Antipodean Whirligig." Just before keeping their promise to repair and improve it, Wignell and Reinagle opened the Chestnut on July 4 to introduce Fullerton as Octavian in *The Mountaineers*, Gondibert in *The Battle of Hexham*, Lord Duke in *High Life below Stairs* and Young Rapid in *A Cure for the Heartache*. Either his roles were suitable or his audiences less critical in the heat of a Philadelphia summer, for Fullerton was encouraged to believe that he would be accepted at the Chestnut. In act II of *High Life below Stairs* on July 17 he danced a minuet with Mrs. Shaw. There were a Spanish fandango after Act III of *The Mountaineers* on July 8, a roundelay and chorus in Act III of *The Battle of Hexham*, and another roundelay and chorus in *High Life below Stairs* on July 17, with Mrs. Oldmixon and Miss Arnold taking the principal parts; but, with Fullerton supposedly launched, the managers ended the four-night season on July 27.

As for Robertson, his arrival in town resulted in a miniature war of the theatres. With Barrett and Placide, he announced a three-nights' engagement to open at the South Street on August 10, although a detachment from the Chestnut Street company, with the consent of the managers, was advertising a summer season to begin at the same theatre on August 7. Happily for Philadelphians an armistice brought a merger of the groups and one of history's oddest show men treated the town to his "ground and lofty tumbling," his hair-raising leaps over the fixed bayonets of twenty soldiers or through a barrel of fire, and to his "whirligig" act. Standing on his head in what looked like the crown of an old felt hat covered with black lead, Robertson would whirl like a top, "without the assistance of his hands," at a rate of 250 times a minute, "fireworks attached to the different parts of his body." Goggle-eyed witnesses could only perceive a perpendicular object, like the axis of a wheel, going round with immense rapidity.

Robertson's versatility was almost as astonishing. He appeared with McDonald in the "laughable scene" of *Roly Poly* and in his own comic pantomime of *Harlequin Recruit*. He gave lifelike imitations of the songs of the robin, thrush, skylark, and nightingale that would have delighted the Philadelphia nature-lovers, Wilson and Peale. He also whistled a grand overture, accompanied by the band.

After a benefit on September 21, Robertson went South, where he broke his neck in attempting to execute one of his dangerous feats.

With Robertson came a prodigy, Master Lynch of Ireland,

one of a line including Master Whale, whose victories on the field of honor, sabre upraised and tiny foot on the breast of a six-foot actor, were to raise a derisive shout at the Chestnut; Master Payne, later a celebrated playwright and the author of "Home, Sweet Home," but an acceptable Hamlet at eighteen; and Master Burke, the "Irish Roscius," who at twelve regaled the Chestnut's patrons with close to thirty roles in eleven nights. Lynch's specialty was "The Old Woman of Eighty," a song he offered on August 10 and 17 and repeated "by request" on September 16, 21, and October 2. On September 25 he sang a "comic song" in the character of a country boy, a type of entertainment then popular. There were other songs by Miss Arnold on August 14 and October 2. Dances included "The Highland Fling," a variety of strathspeys, reels, etc., by Francis on September 7 and the *minuet de la cour* and a new gavotte by Master Harris and Miss Arnold on September 25.

It was an ambitious program for the time of year, offering three Philadelphia premières, *The Way to Keep Him*—with an additional scene by the author and a new prologue as spoken by Cain, on October 2, the season's final night—*The London Hermit,* and the American *Bunker Hill.* The South Street, with a drop curtain by the versatile André still in its possession, was an appropriate setting for an historical play of another martyr; and the artists rose to the occasion with some elaborate scenes of the American Camp, the Charles River, and the battle itself. The director collaborated with a final scene "imitative of the celebrated picture by Turnbull of the death of General Warren."

Its interior renovated, the Chestnut opened for the fall season on October 14, 1801, with a trifle in verse entitled *The Election.* It had nothing to do with Jefferson's accession to power. The candidates are Comedy and Tragedy, who contend for the palm of public favor. Pantomime enters the contest; but Mercury, acting as judge, settles the dispute by assigning a role to each.

In the season, comedy's role were thirty-seven plays. There were eleven farces and sixteen tragedies. There were six national premières, including *The Poor Gentleman,* Colman the Younger's celebrated comedy, and eleven Philadelphia premières, one of them Fawcett's tuneful and cleverly constructed *Obi or Three-Fingered Jack,* with its revelation of the voodoo practiced by the West Indian negroes, its theme of terror, and its dominant character of Jack, long a scourge of the island of Jamaica.

The Poor Gentleman, first produced at Covent Garden February 11, 1800, was to have a season's record of six performances and *Obi* of six; but the managers were heading into stormy water. Although Oldschool in the *Port Folio* pronounced Fullerton "good" as Lt. Worthington, the British gentleman and ill-appreciated veteran (an especially sympathetic role only eighteen years after the Revolution), he was proving no substitute for Cooper. He was "more vehement than Petruchio demanded," Oldschool reports for October 23; and "his voice was too loud." It was harsh, unmusical and monotonous on October 26; and, on November 11, his interpretation of Colonel Epaulette in *A Trip to Fontainbleau,* "had nothing French in air, accent or gesture." Fullerton drew hisses when he "burlesqued Hotspur," on January 8. His voice was "unusually monotonous" in a part, opines Oldschool, above the actor's powers. Demonstrations against Fullerton distracted the performers who appeared in the same scenes with him and Wood, a brother actor, reports that Fullerton's "terror and agony on entering the stage was truly pitiable."

With the election of Jefferson, the aristocrat with leanings toward the common man, the patrons of pit and gallery were obviously feeling their Republican oats. In any event they were becoming more vocal and assertive. The remarks they pointed at the box-holders, occasionally given to loud conversation, were only measurably justified; and they stood in the private passages leading to the front boxes (so the managers complained), smoked cigars in defiance of a safety rule and, if leaving early, gave away their return checks. It was inevitable that Fullerton should become their butt and as inevitable that he should find the role insupportable. His last appearance, on January 29, as L'Abbe de L'Epee in *Deaf and Dumb,* was less of an ordeal than usual; but, after brooding for nearly a week, Fullerton left his lodgings at midnight, his hat drawn down over his eyes. Gibbons, master tailor of the Chestnut's wardrobe, found it on the Vine Street dock the morning of February 4; and he gave the alarm leading to the recovery of Fullerton's body from the nearby waters.

While deprecating the treatment given Fullerton, Oldschool found much to censure in the performances of some of the other players. Jones, recently of the Boston Theatre, "fell short of Cooper," on October 19, as Romeo. In *The School for Prejudice,* on November 4, Mrs. Oldmixon made the character of the old maid "too awful" and several of the performers were imperfect in their lines. Two nights later Mrs. Whitlock was "sometimes too vehement" as Jane Shore.

But a better interpretation, Oldschool admits, would have gone for little, as a "violent disturbance" occurred in the theatre as Cain was "pronouncing the moral over" Jane's body. "Some one in a front box sprung from his seat, exclaiming that the gallery was falling," despite the fact it had been rebuilt to prevent a concentration of people in any one part of the building. Cries of fire added to the confusion. People in the boxes darted into the pit and several ladies so forgot themselves as to rush on to the stage. Patrons knew that all lights were "permanently fixed" and carefully guarded, but a "love of mischief" may have prompted the alarm.

After the panic had subsided, Oldschool reports that Bernard, as Shac-a bac in *Blue Beard,* added lines of his own, degrading "his talents in buffoonery"; and Jones' petite, pretty-faced wife, James Wallack's sister, "acted languid" as Fatima and "varied her tones scarcely at all." Her voice was better on November 9, but not her acting. "Cain did not know his part." On November 11, Jones as Osmyn in *The Mourning Bride* was "disappointing." On November 18, Cain's song as the galley slave in *The Purse* was "deficient in pathos and strength." On December 9 Mrs. Francis, though good in "flippant parts," was "cold and languid" as the Countess of Nottingham in *The Earl of Essex.*

But the favorable criticism outweighed the unfavorable. As Peggy in *The Country Girl,* on October 19, Mrs. Jones was "a hit." She dangled her arms, looked gawky, turned her toes in, talked broad Hampshire in a voice "plaintive and expressive"; and her articulation was especially "good." In *The Spanish Barber* on October 26 Bernard and Warren were "a riot." Bernard, who was "cool and easy" as Lizard in *The Secret* on November 2 "excited laughter." Mrs. Merry's song, as Rosa, was "sweetly sung"; and her "speaking voice was fine, too." Her "artless" manner drew tears at the end. Cain was a spirited Henry, Warren as Dorville correct and respectable (as always), Wood witty and animated, and Mrs. Oldmixon "calmly assured as the teacher at Mrs. Monsoon's boarding school." On November 6 Wignell, though recently ill, played a spirited Hastings in the unfortunate performance of *Jane Shore.* In *The Mourning Bride* on November 11, Mrs. Merry as Almeria was "wonderful," and Mrs. Whitlock, too, except that, in the scene with Osmyn, her emotion "burst forth rather as a jealous wife than the haughty Zara"—though it may have been in an effort to arouse Jones from the listless way in which he was playing his part. On the same night Bernard's "easy, unabashed impudence" as Lackland in *A Trip to Fontainbleau,* was "laughable," Blissett as the taylor "comic as usual," and Warren, Mrs. Francis and Mrs. Oldmixon "polished as the family of Throgmorton Street"—compensation for the inadequacy of poor Fullerton. Jones as well as Fullerton outdid himself in *Speed the Plough* on November 16. His interpretation of Frederic was "just and accurate" and Oldschool reports that the audience "applauded well." Some critics ridiculed and mocked Jones' "tones, which appears to excite terror in acting," thought Oldschool. "To this we attribute his failure in Osmyn." But Jones' voice in Frederic "displayed all its flexibility and variety." In a few instances his articulation was hurried and indistinct, but this was Jones' only error on this evening. Miss Westray's Emily was "charmingly" played, Mrs. Oldmixon as Lucretia was good as usual, Warren was perfect as Sir Robert Bramble. In general, writes Oldschool, he "achieves high excellence and never offends in any part." Bernard as Ollapod was "irresistibly ludicrous without being extravagant." On December 7 Bernard's Sheva in *The Jew* was "excellent" and in *St. David's Day* Warren and Bernard were "very merry." In *The Earl of Essex* on December 9 Mrs. Whitlock was "fine" as a "haughty and impetuous Elizabeth" and Mrs. Merry as the Countess of Rutland held her "usual resistless sway over the audience." The ailing Wignell played the arduous part of Essex with "spirit and propriety." In *Douglas,* on December 11, Oldschool commended Jones and Mrs. Whitlock; and, in *Il Bondocani,* Bernard for his Cadi, Wood for his Hassan, Warren for his Chebib, and Jones for his Haroun Al Raschid. Cain supported the character of Abdallah "with much spirit," though "his song was very deficient in energy." In *The Battle of Hexham,* on December 16, Bernard as Gregory Gubbins "diverted the audience" with his "quaint jokes and coward tremor" but Oldschool tempers his praise with the comment that the manner in which Bernard sang his merry song made the audience forget the "moral of the burthen" and they were "immoderate in their applause." Oldschool commends Miss Westray for the "vivacity and archness" of her performance, most likely of Augusta, in *A Wedding in Wales* on February 8, and again for her impersonation on March 19 of a "fair Quaker" in *Windsor Wags,* in which she "looked and sang sweetly," although he did "not notice in" the "action" of Poe's future mother, "that improvement which" he "had anticipated from her early essays." But Bernard, as Quotem, "was admirable; and his song, and his journal of the multifarious employments of the day, were equally irresistible."

The stock actors, the "rushlights," were improving by the performance. On November 27 Wood as Young Pranks in *The London Hermit* was "particularly successful," thought Oldschool; "the play went off cheerfully" and "people left" the theatre "smiling". On December 9 Wood played Southampton in *The Earl of Essex* "with feeling and energy." Oldschool even compared him favorably with Cooper as Rolla when Wood played the role on March 10. In *Henry IV, I,* on January 8, Warren was "good" as Falstaff though surrounded by players whose performances were mediocre; and, on March 5, the cast as a whole won laurels in a "well acted" interpretation of *Folly As It Flies,* a comedy about the French quack who could cure "toutes les maladies et plusieurs autres." But the company suffered a disappointment in a lack of patronage for the eight plays of Shakespeare presented in the season. Despite "very good" portrayals of Mrs. Whitlock as Portia (Oldschool called her eyes "especially expressive") and Bernard as Shylock, there was a "scarce audience" to witness *The Merchant of Venice* and "scanty audiences" were present for *Cymbeline, The Merry Wives of Windsor,* and *Macbeth,* with Mrs. Siddons' sister, Mrs. Whitlock, "excellent" in the leading feminine role; but Oldschool reports that "Shakespeare didn't pay" and there were "too many parties" given on theatre nights. Because of the parties, says Oldschool, *Joanna of Montfaucon,* lavishly produced on February 5 and a Covent Garden counterattraction to the "splendid spectacle," adds Oldschool, of *Pizarro,* drew a "house nearly deserted." The cold of winters that could freeze over the Delaware and make it possible to draw sledges loaded with oak for the stoves of the city over the solid ice of the river drove the ailing Mrs. Oldmixon from the draughty stage of the Chestnut, at her benefit on March 20, in Act IV of *Three Weeks after Marriage. Reparation* had to be substituted for *The Enraged Musician,* in which she was billed to sing.

The Managers, of course, made their complement of mistakes, overplaying the popularity of *Speed the Plough* by substituting it for *The Earl of Essex* on December 4 and letting Francis announce, for his benefit on March 24, a procession in honor of the ratification of the constitution of the United States that was to be only a mechanical parade of cardboard figures six inches in height although an advertisement in the newspapers of the previous day called upon "all persons concerned in the grand procession to attend a full rehearsal, after this evening's performance shall be concluded." On March 10 and 22 Wignell & Reinagle also made the mistake of offering bills so lengthy that they emptied the boxes and most of the pit and led the gallery to yawn in wonder at when they would end.

But there were crowded houses and fashionable audiences, too; on February 8 for *The Wedding in Wales* and even, on March 10, for *Pizarro,* with Mrs. Merry, "Corinthian column of the dramatic temple," acting in her benefit as Elvira on March 10. Discriminating patrons were grateful to the managers for bringing to Philadelphia the latest from London in *What Would the Man Be At?* (presented in

America for the first time) and the farce of *Windsor Wags.*

Meanwhile the artists had been wielding their brushes to good effect. Oldschool felt they destroyed the illusion by bringing the pyre too far forward in *The Widow of Malabar;* but, after seeing *Hercules and Omphale,* first produced in America on February 22, he writes: "Upon the whole, we think that we may venture to affirm that, for elegant scenery and splendid pageantry, this pantomime has been, hitherto, unrivalled on the American stage." The artists had contrived for the piece a "shower" of Olympian fire. For *Obi* they created a "view of extensive plantations," an "apartment in the planter's house," the "inside of an Obi woman's cave," a "bay in Jamaica", and, for Act III of *Adelmorn,* an effective "vision" as it appeared to the outlaw.

For the music lovers there were Mrs. Oldmixon's song "Ah Hapless is the Maiden" in *The Spanish Barber* which, says Oldschool, they "loudly applauded" on October 26, the "pleasing" harmonies of *The Shipwreck* on November 4, Mrs. Jones' sweet voice as Fatima on November 6, and in "The Day of Marriage" on November 23 and April 5 (after Act III of *The Castle Spectre*). There were "The Blue Bells of Scotland," sung by Mrs. Oldmixon in *St. David's Day* which, on December 7, writes Oldschool, proved a "delight to the amateur" with its genuine Welsh airs of remote antiquity. On December 11 there were also a "difficult song" in *Il Bondocani,* which Miss Arnold sang "with energy and effect", and Mrs. Jones' "sweet flowing measures" which "charmed all hearts." There were songs and musical accompaniments in *Obi* on December 26; and Mrs. Oldmixon, on March 1, sang the Welsh air of "Owen," accompanied on the harp by Mr. Chateaudun, at the end of Act I of *St. David's Day*. On March 20 Master Lynch sang "The Old Woman of Eighty" and Miss Arnold a "favorite song" on March 22. There were a "Welsh overture" (to *St. David's Day*) and a "Masonic prelude" on the same night. After

Hamlet, on March 26, Master Lynch sang a song in the character of a country boy; and, on April 5, Mrs. Jones the ballad of "The Nosegay Girl" and "The Day of Marriage."

For devotees of the dance there was a rural dance composed by Francis on November 25 and a double hornpipe interpreted by Durang and Miss Solomons on April 2. These were in addition to the dances offered as a part of the performances. A delegation of Shawnee and Delaware chiefs exhibited their terpsichorean art on March 8 in their "Corn Piece" and other country dances and their war dance, in which an eyewitness years later recalled the Indians as having been "so terribly in earnest that in their furor piece after piece of their scanty drapery became so unfixed and disarranged as to occasion the flight of several ladies from the boxes. A punster, hearing some doubts expressed as to whether they were real Indians, declared he was sure they were, at least as far as the "Show Knees" were concerned.

For good measure there were recitations including a prologue to *Life* by the aging Wignell on January 1, an epilogue to *The Wedding in Wales* by Bernard on February 8, "A Dissertation on Hobby Horses," also by Bernard on March 20, and Dryden's "Ode on St. Cecilia's Day" by Jones after *The Castle Spectre* on April 5.

Near the season's end Green, a member of the 1793 company, returned from a tour of Virginia, appeared as Young Rapid in *A Cure for the Heartache* on March 12 and in Cooper's role of Osmond in *The Castle Spectre;* but Oldschool reports that Green's voice was "weak," he was evidently "used to a smaller stage" and that he suffered in comparison with Cooper. The sweet-voiced Mrs. Jones appeared as Rosina and Cooper as Hamlet on April 4, as a fillip to a season that had lacked a leading tragedian to fill the Shakespearean roles.

4

A Great Manager Passes
1802-1803

THE SCENE is the South Street Theatre on the night of July 7, 1802. A detachment of the Chestnut Street company is assembled for a short summer season which, except for the inclemency of the weather, would have opened on the day after Independence Day. "Jefferson's March," composed by Reinagle, has just been played and the curtain risen on *The Federal Oath* or *The Independence of 1776*. On the stage a number of peasants are represented as gathering to celebrate the day. An old man and woman serve cakes and mead and there is a dance by Master Harris, Miss K. Solomon, Miss Hunt, Miss Scriven, and others, when suddenly a storm is heard to approach. The women flee; the men get their arms and exit in different directions. Suddenly Peace appears in a white, flowing robe, a garland on her head, an olive branch in her hand. Songs follow, "My Fine Shepherds of Late" by Arne, and " 'Tis Liberty, Dear Liberty" by Handel, from the sweet-voiced Mrs. Jones, who assumes the character of Peace. Miss Solomons plays the part of a Spirit.

It is symbolical of the States' struggle for unity. In the second scene appear a pedestal inscribed with Patrick Henry's immortal "Liberty or Death" and a transparent painting representing Liberty, Columbia, and Justice, flanked by soldiers and sailors. The orchestra plays "The President's March"; then the General, impersonated by Jones, advances and delivers an ode to the United States. Members of the company fill the roles of officers—Warren, Bernard, Wood, Cain, Usher, Blissett, Francis, Hallam. There follows "Washington's March," with Milbourne as an Indian Chief. Six principal officers march around the stage, draw their swords and place them on the altar. Each, then, takes his sword from the altar, kneels down, kisses the blade, and repeats the words, "Liberty or death." Once the oath has been taken, there are three "huzzas" and a national invocation and chorus with the music by Carr.

The theatre reflects the passing of the old order. Washington's lady, Martha, has followed him in death on May 22, 1802; and the States, banded together, are awakening to new responsibilities at home and abroad. On the seas they have been used as a shuttlecock in the French-English game of battledore; and Napoleon, despite misadventures in San Domingo, is curbing the expansion of the West by his continued possession of Louisiana, a territory then extending from the Mississippi River to the Rocky Mountains and from New Orleans to the Canadian Boundary.

Threats from abroad, of course, have only served to impart a finer temper to the sword of confederation. Victories of her infant navy in the undeclared war of about three years ending February 3, 1801, have aroused in America a new sense of power often expressed in the theatre bills. On January 1, 1803, the managers offer *The Corsair* or *The Tripolitan Robbers,* a pantomime "new modelled from" *Obi* and about the Barbary Pirates, and, on February 18, an ode to American Liberty, as spoken by Hodgkinson. On March 14 they scheduled *The Enterprise* or *A Wreath for American Tars,* an "entertainment of dialogue, singing and spectacle," a direct appeal to the dawning pride in the naval forces and particularly in the 12-gun schooner that had captured eight French vessels and, on August 1, 1801, acquired new laurels in a battle with the 14-gun *Tripoli.* It was a battle worthy of the best efforts of the scene painters. Twice the corsairs had lowered their flag and twice fired treacherously on the Americans about to take possession. But realizing the Americans had decided to sink their ship, the enemy had thrown their flag into the sea and abjectly surrendered. The artists provided a view of the Mediterranean "with the chase at a distance until the ships are discovered at close action. With the different manoevres," runs an advertisement, "until the *Tripolitan* strikes, is dismasted and turned adrift." As late as May 19, 1800, Philadelphians had been reminded that pirates still were operating in even closer waters when three of the gentry were hanged on an island off the Market Street pier; and with the Bashaw of Tripoli still defying an American fleet, the Chestnut's patrons doted on scenes so evocative of the patriotic spirit.

At the end of their brief summer season on July 19, the South Street contingent had appealed to this spirit in presenting the tragedy of *Bunker Hill* or *The Death of General Warren* and had added *Red Cross Knights* to *The Federal Oath* as another Philadelphia première. There was a "regal banquet" in Act IV of the new play and Mrs. Jones sang "The Soldier Tired of War's Alarms." But the weather was sultry and the theatre uncomfortable, despite the use of an expensive "front cloth" designed and executed by Holland and Milbourne. Worse still, it was fever weather; and Yellow Jack was again rearing his ghastly head. On July 15 Elizabeth Drinker wrote in her diary, "Great talk of yellow fever

—many moving out of town," and on September 2 the Health Board "earnestly intreat ye citizens to avoid all unnecessary intercourse with the sick; and those who have retired into the country are advised to remain until they can return with safety." In 1802 the fever was to kill 835 persons.

Under the circumstances the fall season opened as late as December 13. The weather now turned savagely cold and the guerdon of a "bushel of oysters for the horse" seemed a reasonable price for a seat near the fireplace of an inn. There were changes and postponements. On January 5 *Lock and Key* was substituted for *The Rival Soldiers,* deferred until January 7 for what was obviously the usual reason, the illness of a principal performer; and the bill of January 14 was delayed until January 15 owing to storms. *The Shipwreck,* scheduled for February 9, was abandoned for *Rosina* when Bernard fell ill, a night when the company exhibited the warmheartedness of their profession in devoting a part of their receipts to the relief of the victims of a fire at Portsmouth, N. H.

The rigors of the winter robbed the theatre of the services of Oldschool who, despite declining health, had been writing some of his most pungent criticism. He had been too ill to see Cooper bring the previous season to a brilliant close; but he had commended Cain for his "arduous," "respectable," though "not completely successful" Hamlet, and Mrs. Merry for her excellent Ophelia, Wood for his Tangent in *The Way to Get Married,* a role the actor Moreton might have considered his own but which, in Wood's hands, "got universal applause." Mrs. Merry as Julia was "attractive" and Miss Westray as Olivia in *A Bold Stroke for a Husband* "played with vivacity and spirit." Oldschool's criticisms were to be missed and future historians to have no check against last-minute changes in the bills as published.

But the weather was less of an ordeal than the riots occasioned by the strong political sentiments of the day which,

A Great Manager Passes

equally gusty and uncertain, vented their spleen on Bernard, who offered a toast to President Jefferson while playing in *The Deaf Lover* on January 17. There were hisses from the audience and fulminations from the Federalist press. Competition, too, was becoming a problem. Rannie, "professor of legerdemain and ventriloquism," and Swann, riding master and farrier, were drawing patronage from the Chestnut. The "Italian Fantoccina," a puppet show, billed as making its American début, was running through a series of successful performances at the South Street before moving to Ignace's Dancing Academy at 70 S. 4th Street.

Yet an even severer blow than loss of patronage due to stormy weather, unruly audiences or attractive competition was about to fall on the Chestnut. It was the death on February 21 of co-manager Wignell who, with Reinagle, had assembled the 1793 troupe and opened the Chestnut in 1794. Only in January he had married Mrs. Merry, widow of the one-time playboy and poet "Della Crusca," dead of a stroke in 1798. Wignell, stockily built and full-blooded, had been injured by a spring-lancet. Grangrene had resulted and the shortish, jaunty figure, hat cocked on one side and swinging a cane, would be gone forever from the scene of his labors. He had acted little in recent years, though his Darby in *The Poor Soldier* and his Joseph Surface had once been a challenge to the most competent players.

Fennell, a member of 1793 company, recalls the last time he "had the pleasure" of seeing Wignell was the night of February 12 "in his private box at the theatre, whither he had invited me to attend the performance of Mr. Hodgkinson in Macbeth. During the play he observed to me that his arm was so painful that he was obliged to request that I would permit him to leave me, and return home . . . From that time I never saw him more."

Writing in the style of his period, Fennell testifies in his *Apology,* a book that reflects *A Groat's Worth of Wit bought with a Million of Repentance,* by the Elizabethan Greene, that:

The four Cornerstones which supported the basis of Mr. Wignell's character were Candor, Truth, Integrity and Honor. Its superstructure was the column of Hope, about which had entwined, as around the Corinthian pillar, the vine of Perseverance, bearing the full blown rose in all its brilliant excellence, and the green leaf in all its sweet complacency; its capital was of the noblest order and of the highest polish.

As a manager, of course, Wignell was well-nigh irreplaceable. Though handicapped by his backers with an expensive music department (albeit directed by Reinagle) and a system of free tickets for the stockholders of the Chestnut, he had helped Reinagle to justify Washington's support of the theatre and, as a good executive, had trained an understudy to take his place—actually two of them, Warren and Wood, who became the "acting managers," under the aegis of Mrs. Wignell and Reinagle, on February 28, assuring the friends of the drama that "every exertion will be made to merit a continuance of their patronage and approbation."

Abaellino, new to Philadelphia, *The Castle Spectre,* and *The Sixty-Third Letter,* also new, had already pleased the Chestnut's patrons; and by the end of the season they were to see thirteen new pieces, three of them presented in America for the first time and including *Henry IV, II,* with Warren in his successful role of Falstaff.

The company had lost the Whitlocks to New York; but Mrs. Barrett, from the theatres of New York and Charleston, had replaced Mrs. Whitlock in some of the heavy roles. Early in the season and prior to a tour abroad, Cooper played Hamlet, Richard, Pierre in *Venice Preserved,* and Macbeth. Later Fennell and Hodgkinson, both from New York, also played Shakespearean and other important roles. Fennell, a giant of six feet six, was a man of cultivation who taught elocution and had lectured at the University of Pennsylvania. Hodgkinson, now appearing at the Chestnut for the first time, was the "Atlas of the American Stage," reputedly playing eighty different roles in a single engagement. He was excellent with Fennell in such plays as *Venice Preserved* and *The Revenge*. On February 16 Hogg of the New York theatre made his bow at the Chestnut as Lord Scratch in *The Dramatist*.

Some of the scenery for the plays represented the best efforts of the artists. It was elaborate for *Henry VIII* and *Sancho Turned Governor,* both new to the town, and for *The Virgin of the Sun;* and in *Alfonso,* another Philadelphia first, a procession of nuns and friars to the shrine of St. Juan, to the accompaniment of singing by Mrs. Oldmixon, Mrs. Jones, and others, and a "garden and terrace leading to the palace of Alfonso, terminating with a beautiful cascade," were impressive. In Act V of the same tragedy, there were a "cavern partially lighted by lamps" and, in the middle, "folding doors guarded by iron bars." During the scene a mine blew up with a loud explosion and the back part of the vault burst into flames. On March 16, at his benefit, as if to make amends for the folly he had committed the previous year, Francis enlisted the aid of Holland in preparing a beautiful setting for *The Tempest,* including a "rocky part of an enchanted island" and in *Harlequin Prisoner* a "Garden of Love" into which Cupid descended for a new "Garland Dance" by the children of the company. In *Harlequin's Almanac* on April 2 there was an "enchanted rose-bush" that blossomed and faded.

The songs were becoming overnumerous, with partisans of the players calling for their favorite melodies. Fox sang on December 31; again on March 9 (specifically "The Post Captain"); on March 14, after *Abaellino,* "The Mid-Watch"; on March 16 a "Masonic" song accompanied by a chorus;

on March 30 a parody written by Bernard on Dibdin's "Tom Tackle" and called "Poll Primrose"; and on April 2 a hunting song. On March 16 there was also "The Masonic Ode" by Brothers Warren, Fox, Robbins, Francis, Reinagle, etc., as sung at the dedication of the Pennsylvania Free-Mason's Hall. On December 31 Mrs. Jones sang the popular "Day of Marriage," repeating it, after *The Belle's Stratagem,* on March 28. On December 31 Mrs. Oldmixon sang the cantata of "Mad Bess," which her admirers liked; and on his benefit night, February 18, Hodgkinson, who had begun his career as a fiddler and singer, contributed the "comic ditty" of "The Group of Lovers or Beauty at her Levee," billed as a "whimsical description of Whiffle (a beau), Jack Bumper, Sammy Simple, Ensign Bluff, Terrence McBrawn, Hezekiah Prim, and Captain Worthy." On March 11 Bernard sang "The Auctioneer," one of his comic repertory; and on April 2 Hallam "explained in song" that there were more tanners than those who made leather. In *Harlequin's Almanac,* on the same night, there was a "glee" of two poor gardeners by Blissett and Fox.

The dances included a "country dance" by the characters, as an accompaniment to a "representation of a ploughing match" in Act II of *Speed the Plough* on January 29; a "characteristic dance" by Master Harris, Master Durang and Miss Hunt in Wolsey's palace in *Henry VIII* on February 2; a minuet in Act II of *The Belle's Stratagem* by Mrs. Jones and Durang on March 28; a mock minuet by Fox and Mrs. Shaw in Act II of *High Life Below Stairs* on March 30; and, on April 1, the *minuet de la cour* by Master Harris and Miss Hunt and the "much admired *pas de trois*" by Master Harris, Master Durang, and Miss Hunt, after *Which Is the Man?*

The season's recitations included, on December 31, "The Comic Tale of Monsieur Tonson," by Green, "Alonzo and

A Great Manager Passes

Imogene," by Cooper, "Giles Jallup and Brown Sally Green," by Bernard—all three a part of *Melocosmiotes*—an occasional address by Wignell, previous to the pantomime on January 1; an ode to American liberty, by the English Hodgkinson, on February 18; an address to the town in the character of Marplot in *The Busybody*, by Bernard on March 9; an epilogue to *Such Things Are,* by Mrs. Oldmixon on March 11; a Masonic address, by "Brother" Fox on March 16; and Bernard's much appreciated "Dissertation on Hobby Horses" after *The Way to Get Married* on March 26.

The end of the season fell on April 4 with a beautifully staged performance of *Harlequin's Almanac,* a pantomime presented in Philadelphia for the first time on April 2. Milbourne directed it, Holland designed the scenery and machinery, and Reinagle furnished the accompanying music. It brought a trying season to a satisfactory close.

Meanwhile, on the stage of history, circumstances were shaping an equally satisfactory denouement for a drama being enacted by a cast of many of the statesmen of the period. They were now in the wings waiting for one of their number, the Emperor Napoleon, to give the cue for their final scene. In 1795 Spain had granted America the privilege of transshipping goods from New Orleans without charge and, though having secretly re-ceded Louisiana to France in 1800, had withdrawn the privilege in 1802. But Napoleon was having trouble on one of the sectors of his far-flung battle for world domination, San Domingo, where yellow fever and the Negro patriot Toussaint L'Ouverture combined to block his ambitious plans. With England once more an enemy, the Emperor suddenly ended the drama on May 2, 1803, by selling Jefferson's deputies all of Louisiana, a territory larger than the American Republic itself, for the sum of $15 million. There were to be plays at the Chestnut and

South Street that must have fitted the mood of rejoicing theatregoers : the indigenously British *John Bull,* the patriotic *Death of General Wolfe, The Tripolitan Prize, Count Benyowski,* and *Liberty in Louisiana,* and the satirical *Bonaparte Mistaken.*

5

First Jefferson and First Melodrama
1803-1804

HIS FIGURE was extremely dwarfish, thin but rather muscular. His complexion was cadaverous. He had large hazel eyes, light hair that was stiff and without a curl, and a large hooked nose. The tout ensemble prepared an audience for something droll; yet, as a contemporary viewed him, he was saturnine if not "hypocondriacal" in disposition. Having decided to be an actor in early youth, he had stuck to the point "like a rusty weather-cock" and become one of the best burletta singers in England. Wood found him in Macready's company at Birmingham on a recruiting trip the new acting manager had undertaken following a decision to remain on the stage, which he had been tempted to desert for a business career. The new performer was Twaits and he first appeared at the Chestnut on December 14, 1803, as Pangloss in *The Heir at Law*. His interpretation of the role was so successful that every print-shop in the city soon displayed his likeness as the good doctor. It was a rare distinction at the time.

But an acquisition even more valuable than Twaits was a comedian from the Park with whom negotiations had been opened prior to Wood's departure for Europe, the second in line of one of the stage's royal families, including the Booths, the Sotherns, and the Drews and Barrimores. The new comedian, Plymouth-born, was the son of an actor-manager; and in 1795 he had come to Boston, where he joined the Federal Street Theatre company. The following year, when he became a member of the John Street company in New York, Dunlap, American stage historian and contemporary, describes him as being a "youth, but even then an artist. Of a small, slight figure, well-formed, with a singular physiognomy, a nose perfectly Grecian, and blue eyes full of laughter, he had the faculty of exciting mirth to as great a degree by power of feature, although handsome, as any ugly-featured low comedian ever seen." Owing to the prejudices of the time which demanded an actor of Cooper's height for tragic roles, the Chestnut's new player was discouraged from attempting them, though his "transitions from jocular dialogue to a few lines of sentiment," in the words of a witness, were "thrillingly beautiful" and disclosed that he could have worn the buskin as well as the sock.

Such was Joseph Jefferson, who began a long and distinguished career at the Chestnut on December 12, the opening night of its 1803-1804 season. From the beginning his excellence as a comedian and his versatility were recognized. He could play Sir Oliver, Charles Surface, or Crabtree in *The School for Scandal* equally well and he simulated the halting gait of the aged so successfully that once a kind-hearted lady, believing him needy, planned a subscription for him. Jefferson had a strong and mellow tenor which he used to advantage in harmonizing with Twaits and he was an inventor like Thomas Jefferson of Washington and Monticello, whom he came to know only slightly but resembled, it

First Jefferson and First Melodrama 59

was thought, to a marked degree. The actor even bettered the English models for stage machinery and his conflagration scenes were so convincing that theatre "ads." and bills had to warn a possibly jittery public that they were part of the performance.

Bernard had left the Chestnut Street company, having at first decided to return to England and then to go to Boston; but Mrs. Wignell and Reinagle, with a corps of comedians including Blisset, Warren, and Wood in addition to the newcomers, were able to present as many as forty-two farces and comedies in the season of 1803-1804. Mrs. Jefferson, who made her bow at the Chestnut on December 30 as Rosara in *She Would and She Would Not,* was less notable as an actress than as the mother of the second Joseph Jefferson and seven other children, six of whom were players; but Hardinge, a celebrated stage Irishman, and the "tall and elegant" Mrs. Morris, the toast of New York in 1792, docking with Wood November 15, 1803, on the Lewis William, were welcomed, after an absence of four years, for their vocal and instrumental talent. Hardinge's first appearance was as Shiva in *The Jew* on December 16 and Mrs. Morris' —regrettably her only appearance for the season—was as the Widow Brady on March 14 with the original "epilogue" song.

While Wood was searching for talent abroad and the Chestnut Street Company was on its Southern circuit— which from time to time was to include Washington, Alexandria and Baltimore and be the means of holding the company together and of its escape from town at a time when the plague might reappear—an actor named McGinnis opened the South Street with what he termed "A Theatric Lounge." Only seven of its bills are preserved in the records available. On July 27, in addition to songs and recitations, there were scenes from *The Mountaineers, Dr. Last's Examination,* and astonishing feats on the slack wire by Othello, "the Grand

African," performed, as modestly proclaimed, "in a manner surpassing conception." On August 1, there were *Love à la Mode;* "Four and Twenty Fiddlers," a comic song in character by Durang; "The Blue Bells of Scotland," as sung "by a lady" making her first appearance on the South Street stage; and "A Clown's Description of London" as sung by McGinnis. For variety, there were a Spanish Saraband by a "young lady" who danced blindfolded over thirteen eggs and a representation of the Battle of the Nile, made possible by a piece of machinery surpassing "anything of the kind ever exhibited." On August 2 a dancing horse which had performed in the South Street repeated the tricks he had been taught; and again on August 5, prior to his being shipped abroad as a present to the Emperor Napoleon. Fox, whose voice was showing the effects of excessive drinking, sang "The Wounded Huzzar," "Her Mouth Which a Smile," "The Turbanned Turk," and "The Post Captain." There was also a comic song "by a lady," usually the anonym of a person objecting to being classed an actress. McGinnis spoke an occasional prologue written by a gentleman of Philadelphia, Swann demonstrated the six divisions of the exercise of the broad sword and Durang, dressed in character, recited the "favorite" piece of "The Dutchman and His Wife." The only dramatic portions of the bill were the first and last scenes of *The Revenge.*

On August 16, for the benefit of Mrs. McGinnis, there were a pantomime, gymnastic feats, vocal and instrumental music, a pastoral, and a country dance, with performances of *Like Master Like Man* (*Lovers' Quarrels*) and *Patrick's Return* (*The Poor Soldier*). McGinnis' benefit followed on August 20, with scenes from *The Mountaineers,* a performance of *Love à la Mode,* a pantomime by McGinnis, gymnastic feats by a gentleman (this night only), a grand chorus adapted to the occasion in which was introduced a "fancy"

First Jefferson and First Melodrama

pastoral dance. A Country Dance ended the bill, evidently the last of the South Street's entertainments.

There was little competition from the old theatre during the 1803-1804 season. Record exists that on January 7, 1804, Rannie, the ventriloquist, and Manfredi, a tight rope performer, appeared at the South Street, Manfredi offering to "forfeit $1000 that he" was "the only tight rope dancer in the known world." But the Chestnut's managers could have weathered a much severer bid for public favor. They had scheduled for the season four of Shakespeare's plays and, among the pieces to be presented for the first time in Philadelphia, seven that had just been produced in London—three from Drury Lane, two from Covent Garden, and two from the Little Haymarket—and four others that were new in Britain. In *The Marriage Promise* and *The Maid of Bristol* they had plays that scored an immediate success; in *John Bull,* acted four times in 1803-1804 and *A Tale of Mystery,* acted six, a domestic comedy and a new type of drama where "received with most enthusiastic applause and delight" at the Chestnut.

The success of *John Bull* or *An Englishman's Fireside* was surprisingly unexpected. It was thought to be too British and American theatres sometimes changed its variant title to *An Honest Man's Fireside*. Wood had brought the manuscript of the play from England and the universality of its appeal more than justified the price of 1000 pounds that Colman the Younger originally received for it.

A Tale of Mystery, the first "melodrama" ever produced in America, was an adaptation by Thomas Holcroft of Pixérécourt's *Coelina*. It had its American première in New York on March 16, 1803. There were the usual accompaniments of the musical drama in its Philadelphia production—Dr. Busby's original music, with additions by Reinagle—and scenery by Holland, Milbourne, Robbins, and Hugh Reinagle, son of the composer (the last two recently added to the staff of artists). In Act II a "beautiful garden and pleasure grounds, with garlands, festoons, devices and every preparation for a marriage festival" pleased the ladies in the boxes, much given to gardening themselves; and in Act III, a "wild and mountainous country" with "pines and massive rocks," a "rude wooden bridge" connecting them, and a "rugged mill stream in the background" quickened the pulses of the adventure-loving males who witnessed the villain's traditional pursuit of the lily-hearted heroine. There was a characteristic dance composed by Francis in Act II, but what made *A Tale of Mystery* a novelty was its use of music to create a proper mood for the scenes that followed or for a better appreciation of tender or dramatic incidents, in the manner of the melo- or music drama as at first conceived.

The Chestnut's artists prepared their usual settings for *Romeo and Juliet, Paul and Virginia*, a "Gothic saloon" and "gloomy dungeon" for *A Tale of Terror*, a "subterranean cavern" for *The Knights of Calatrava*, and a "grand Winter scene" for *Count Benyowski*, with the stage representing "the cold inhospitable climate of Kamschatka," a type of scene popular at the Chestnut, perhaps because its patrons lived closer to nature in the era before houses were comfortably heated. Advertisements of the bills reveal that the artists painted a vivid picture of the "poverty and misery" of the exiles in this important Kotzebue première; but their most ambitious efforts were expended on the pantomimes, in which the absence of dialogue and the usually romantic story were a challenge to their brushes. In *Raymond and Agnes*, or *The Bleeding Nun*, adapted from Lewis' *The Monk*, one of the seven pantomimes produced this season and now presented for the first time in Philadelphia, the tale of Don Felix' son, moving from castle to forest to hovel, must have been unusually inspiring to Holland, who furnished the scenic background for Aymond's adventures with the banditti, one of whom, Baptist, he killed in self-defense

First Jefferson and First Melodrama 63

before escaping with Agnes, daughter of Count Lindenberg, just finished with her convent education, and Maugarette, Baptist's mistress, who had warned Raymond of a plot against his life. An advertisement of March 9 promises a view, in Act II, Scene I, of the "inside of Lindenberg Castle," to which Raymond returns Agnes. There is to be . . .

[a] picture of the mother of Agnes, the Countess. The Count enters, viewing the picture with agitation, and kneels to implore forgiveness for having murdered her. Agnes [is] brought in by Raymond, who is introduced to the present Countess. [In Scene II there is to be the] chamber of Agnes; portrait of a nun, with a wound upon her breast, a lamp dagger and a rosary upon her arm. Agnes is discovered drawing [announces the advertisement]. Raymond, entering unperceived, throws himself at her feet, and obtains a promise of her hand. He requests an explanation of the picture of the Bleeding Nun. She informs him in a song, 'Tis the resemblance of a Spectre which haunts the castle every fifth year. The Count and Countess approach and in anger order Raymond to quit the castle. Raymond, about to depart, is diverted by the sound of a mandoline [sic]. A paper lowered by Agnes from the castle, containing a drawing of the Nun, with the following scroll: "When the castle bell tolls one, Expect me like the Bleeding Nun." [Scene IV is to be] Outside the castle as before. Raymond enters, the clock strikes one, the gates fly open, the apparition of the Nun comes from the castle, Raymond (supposing it Agnes) follows. Theodore [Raymond's servant] approaching is met by Agnes in the habit of a nun, agitated by the apparent neglect of Raymond. They retire. Raymond following the Spectre (still supposing it Agnes) attempts to embrace it, when suddenly vanishing, a cloud rises from the earth, bearing the following inscription, "Protect the child of the murdered Agnes."

In the final scene Raymond rescues his beloved from the robbers, who have taken her to their cavern; and the piece ends happily. Twaits, who acted in it abroad, assisted Francis in producing the pantomime. Miss Solomon sang a song while playing Antonio, a page to Agnes.

Other incidental music included a dirge as sung in *Romeo and Juliet,* December 19, by Hardinge, Twaits, Jefferson, Fox, Blissett, Mrs. Oldmixon, Miss Westray (who was to become Mrs. Wood on January 30), Mrs. Jefferson, Mrs. Snowden, Mrs. Warren (who was to die on March 10), Mrs. Durang, Mrs. Downie, Miss Hunt, "etc." Twaits sang a comic song as Sylvester Daggerwood, a popular character, on December 21 and March 24. Fox sang a hunting song in the pantomime of *Harlequin Restored* on December 26, and on December 27 Mrs. Oldmixon repeated "The Soldier Tired of War's Alarms" in Scene I of *The Knights of Calatrava.* Hardinge sang the lyrical epilogue to *John Bull* on January 2, 6, 11, and February 8. On March 14 Mrs. Morris sang the original epilogue song to *The Irish Widow.*

In Act II of *Much Ado About Nothing* on March 16 there was a glee by Gillingham, orchestra leader, "Sigh No More, Ladies," sung by Robinson, Blissett, Twaits, and Francis. After *Blue Devils* on the following night Twaits sang "Caleb Quotem's Avocations," "The Doctor's Lament," and "The Town Crier." He also took part in *The Feast of Anacreon* on March 23, with Francis acting as "President," singing two songs (titles unspecified) and, with Reinagle, Blissett, Fox, and Francis, in the glee " 'Twas You, Sir." Fox sang "The Wounded Huzzar" and "Flow, Thou Purple Stream" and Blissett the comic song of "The Learned Pig." As a part of the "feast" there were two other glees, "Fill the Bowl with Rosy Wine" and "Here's a Health to All Good Lasses." On March 26 Twaits sang a comic song with Miss Aaron, Miss Rachael, and Miss Moses, and Reinagle's "Masonic Overture" was repeated.

The incidental dances were a *minuet de la cour* and gavotte danced by Master Harris and Miss Hunt in an Act I masquerade in *Romeo and Juliet* on December 19; a hornpipe

The *"Cradle of Culture"* opposite Independence Hall,
often called the *"Cradle of Liberty"*

Mrs. William Francis
(*minor roles*)
as Miss Harlow

Alexander Reinagle
(*co-manager, composer,
and orchestra leader*)

Master
John Howard Payne
(*prodigy and tragedian*)

William Wood
(*co-manager and
comedian*)

Mrs. William Warren
(*a Lady Macbeth and Ophelia*)

William Francis
(*comedian, dancer, and pantomimist*)
as Sir George Thunder

by T. Worrell on December 26; a pas de trois by Masters Durang and Harris and Miss Hunt on December 27 in Scene I of *The Knights of Calatrava* and a "grand Spanish fandango" at its conclusion. On December 30 a variety of reels and strathspeys were introduced in *The Scheming Milliners* by Master Durang, Miss Solomon, and Miss Hunt. There were "characteristic dances" in Act II of *A Tale of Mystery* on January 20 and of *The Tripolitan Prize* on March 7. On February 1, at the end of Act II of *The Mountaineers,* there was a Spanish fandango; and a "country dance" by the characters to accompany the ploughing match in *Speed the Plough* on February 25. After *Secrets Worth Knowing,* on March 9, there was a Scotch reel by Masters Harris and Durang and Miss Hunt; and, after *Richard III* on March 19, "The Jockey Hornpipe" by the same trio. On March 28, in Scene III of *Paul and Virginia,* there was a "characteristic dance" by Jefferson and Masters Harris, Durang, and Jefferson.

In the season ending April 3, 1804, there seems to have been only one scheduled recitation, "A Dialogue between a Fop and a Master Mason" on March 26, with Warren, on the occasion of his benefit, playing Level (A Master Mason) and Cain playing the Fop. There was also a eulogy on masonry. The budget of American pieces presented was equally slim: *The Wheel of Truth,* a poor farce by Fennell, and *Two Per Cent,* billed as "an entire new interlude."

6

History Takes a Bow
1804-1805

ON MONDAY, July 16, 1804, the inside columns of Philadelphia's American Daily Advertiser were edged in black. Muffled bells had tolled the previous Saturday and members of the Cincinnati were wearing black crape on their arms. Alexander Hamilton was dead. People felt that the forty-seven year old soldier and statesman had actually been murdered in his duel with Aaron Burr. The event was overshadowed, however, by another of major consequence. This was the Louisiana purchase, the importance of which America was just beginning to grasp. "Soldiers out today," Elizabeth Drinker had written in her *Journal* on May 12. "The people are rejoicing upon the acquisition of Louisiana."

In a short Summer season at the South Street, running from June 25 to July 18, a contingent from the Chestnut Street on July 4 reflected the popular fervor in a new play out of Charleston, James Workman's *Liberty in Louisiana,* and an oration by Wood "in honor of Louisiana and the United States." There was also an appeal to America's newly-born pride in her Navy just bringing the Barbary pirates to book. The South Street "exhibited a transparent painting representing Liberty, Columbia and Justice, with Naval columns in honor of Captain Decatur and his brave associates" who had burnt and scuttled the *Philadelphia* (a feat Lord Nelson is said to have pronounced "the most bold and daring act of the age") ; and, on July 6, as a conclusion to *A New Wreath for American Tars,* a "representation of the burning" of the frigate "under the batteries of Tripoli by gallant American seamen." *Bunker Hill,* another patriotic piece, had been acted earlier in the same season; and in the season opening at the Chestnut December 3, 1804, "The Constitution Glee," perhaps a sly reference to the un-Constitutional way in which Jefferson had acquired the new territory, was sung on March 11. Two nights later there was billed a "new patriotic song in praise of the gallant Commodore Preble and his brave tars, who so gallantly distinguished themselves in the different attacks on Tripoli." A "young gentleman of Philadelphia" wrote its words, Reinagle composed its music, and Hardinge sang the song. On March 22 *Arthur and Emmeline,* a made-over masque with the chauvinistic subtitle, *The Prospect of Columbia's Future Glory,* placed Merlin in the role of explaining "to King Arthur the progress of the American Nation from her infancy to her present power and a prophetic view of future glory." There was a sequence of five scenes, each of them introduced, in the manner of the newly popular "melodrama," by music establishing their mood—from Indian, through Spanish and British music, to "Washington's March" and "Yankee Doodle." On March 25 Hardinge sang a new patriotic song, "The Tars of Columbia"; and, for March 27, and Holland's benefit, the artists prepared, as a finale to *American Tars in Tripoli,* a "grand Panorama of the exact situation of the Engagement with the Tripolitans."

From published advertisements theatregoers could anticipate:

[the] plan of the cloth; commencing at the left hand of the Picture is Gun Boat No. 4, commanded by Captain Decatur, with his colours flying over the Tripolitan, which he has taken, and bearing down to the assistance of Lieut. Trip who is engaged on board of the Tripolitan, his own boat having left him and his Brave followers. No. 2, Lieut. James Decatur shot by a Tripolitan (who had struck his colour to him) when about to take possession of his Prize. No. 1, Captain Somers. No. 5, Lieut. Bainbridge upon one of the Rocks with part of his Latteen Yard shot away. No. 3, Lieut. Blake just getting into the engagement. In the front of the Picture to the right is the Constitution frigate, and Syren brig coming in for orders. In the background will be seen the Crown Battery, with a small Red Colour flying. Adjoining, on the right, is the bashaw's Castle—three spires of Mosques, one of which [is] shot away by the Constitution frigate. The whole to conclude with a Grand Transparency in Honour of the Officers lost on the occasion.

The bustling artists were wielding their brushes effectively. For the same night Holland, the principal painter, aided by Milbourne, Robbins, and H. Reinagle, prepared a series of American scenes as an appropriate introduction to *American Tars in Tripoli*. The series, which was interspersed with songs and dances, began with a view of Philadelphia from the Penn Treaty oak. It was followed by "Caleb's Quotem's Avocations," sung by Twaits, and Francis' dance of *Sailors on Shore*. The second view was of the water works in Center Square, later the site of Philadelphia's City Hall. Twaits then sang "Tid-re-I." A view of Baltimore followed and a comic song, "Marriage Is a Lottery," by Blissett. The fourth view was of the great falls of the Potomac, spreading the entire width of the stage. A "national overture" by Reinagle stirred the pulses of the listening theatregoers. A fifth and

History Takes a Bow

final view was of the natural bridge in Virginia. It was followed by *Irish Hay-Makers,* a dance by Francis. The views were shown again and the songs repeated on March 29.

On April 1 the views were once more shown, with Twaits singing "I Say, My Hearts, Why There's Your Work"; a repetition of *Sailors on Shore;* Robbins singing "Bright Beaming Star"; and Blissett "What a Woman Is Like." Francis' "Garland" dance ended the artistic interlude. On April 3, the final night of the season, it was repeated between the acts of *The Way to Get Married,* but with the view of the water works eliminated and without the songs and dances. The panorama of the engagement with the Tripolitans was exhibited again.

But it was such a pantomime as *Raymond and Agnes* of the previous season that afforded the artists their greatest opportunity. This was *La Perouse,* presented for the first time in Philadelphia on December 27, 1804, with the original music by Moorhead and Davy and the orchestral parts by Reinagle. Its Crusoe-like story, with its additional theme of a mutual bond of affection that arises between a man and a beast (a chimpanzee) who save each other's lives, is melodramatic and conventional; and even a *deus ex machina* in the form of a "party of marines" is used to save the situation at its conclusion. But it moves from wreck-strewn beach, to the interior of a cave, to a "natural grotto," to a frozen lake, and to "mountainous country," with the opportunity for snowscape effects so beloved to the Chestnut's patrons and the artists reveled in the scope it gave them while the audiences doted on such hair-raising scenes as La Perouse's attempted suicide, in which lightning strikes a dirk from his grasp, and especially in the gory denouement, in which he escapes death at the stake with the help of the chimpanzee, who slips a pistol into his hand. Music, scenery, and the antics of Jefferson in the role of the beast combined to make the pantomime so popular that *La Perouse* was presented five times, more often than any other piece.

In the season, however, no effort was made to truckle to popular taste. Among the new offerings, in addition to *La Perouse,* were four comedies, three farces, a musical farce, a musical drama, an opera, a tragedy (*Cleone,* given its American première on February 20), a "masque"—*Arthur and Emmeline*—and an operatic farce. Among the bills were nine of Shakespeare's plays and Garrick's "entertainment of music, dialogue and spectacle, *The Shakespeare Jubilee,* honoring the Bard." Its music consisted of "The Jubilee Song," "The Warwickshire Thief" sung by Blissett and Francis, "The Mulberry Tree," by Francis and Cain, and "Sweet Willy O," by Mrs. Oldmixon. There was a pageant in its second act "exhibiting the most prominent characters in Shakespeare's plays."

Cooper's return from a successful engagement in London made this ambitious program possible. He played Hamlet, Richard, Othello, Shylock, Macbeth, Romeo, and Benedick (all in a little over three weeks); and Warren, soon to rival Sir John in girth and already picking his way cautiously over the city's icy streets, contributed his memorable portrait of Falstaff in *Henry IV, I,* and *The Merry Wives of Windsor.*

New players joined the company. The itinerant McKenzie, who had once acted at the John Street Theatre, excellent in Scottish roles, bowed as Peregrine and Seymour of the New York theatre as John Burr in *John Bull* on December 3, 1804. His wife first appeared as Fanny in *A House to be Sold* on December 7. A fourth player, Taylor, bowed as Lindsay in *The Sailor's Daughter* on December 10.

Unlike the Park, which closed with the bankruptcy of Dunlap on February 22, the Chestnut was prospering. Story, a comedian from the London and Charleston theatres, had opened the Southwark for a performance of *The Point of*

Honor and *The Spoiled Child,* with the assistance of young gentlemen, otherwise unidentified, "who have lately performed in this place"; but it was only for the night of October 15. Entertainments rivaling the Chestnut's consisted for the most part of exhibitions of "waxen figures," a chance to see "an African lion of large size," a dancing horse, or to emulate Noah by sitting in an armchair placed in the mouth of a whale that had been caught in the Delaware.

The Chestnut deserved its monopoly. Its music department, which matched its dramatic, was indefatigable under Reinagle in producing incidental music and overtures. For the première of *The Wife of Two Husbands* on March 1 Reinagle, Carr, and Taylor collaborated in a "miscellaneous" overture which contained several solos for the French horn, played by Michault. Even in the brief summer season the songs had been numerous. In the masque of *The Temple of Flora,* on June 27, "The Masquerade Song" had been sung by Mrs. Oldmixon; "Feyther and I or Country Courtship" by Twaits; and "The Birth, Christening, Marriage and Other Family Misfortunes of Mister Dennis Brulgruddery, Showing How He Was Born One Day, Named After the House Dog, Married Once Too Soon, Once Too Late" by Hardinge. "The Country Club" was sung by Jefferson; and there was a glee, "Here's A Health to All Good Lasses," with a "finale" and dance. On July 6 the "Lyrical Epilogue" to *John Bull* and on July 9 the Brulgruddery song were sung by Hardinge. On July 18 a comic song by Twaits accompanied his interpretation of Sylvester Daggerwood. *John Bull's* "Lyrical Epilogue" was repeated by Hardinge on December 3 and February 16. On January 12 in Act II of *Abaellino,* there was vocal and instrumental music by the singers, Mrs. Oldmixon, Seymour, and Robbins and by Gillingham, the leader of the orchestra; also a "favorite" glee, "O Lady Fair" by Mrs. Oldmixon, Jefferson, and Robbins.

On January 18 as part of a funeral procession in Act V of *Romeo and Juliet* there was a "solemn dirge"; and, on January 19 the "comic parody" of "Giles Jallup and Brown Sally Green" by Jefferson; "Captain Wattle and Miss Rose" in the role of Sylvester Daggerwood; and another "comic song" by Twaits. In Act II of *Much Ado About Nothing* on January 21 the glee of "Sigh No More, Ladies" was sung by Robbins, Blissett, Twaits, and Francis. Other songs by Twaits included "Feyther and I" at the end of Act IV of *The Clandestine Marriage* on March 9; "Poor Thomas Day" —with Jefferson and Blissett—on March 11; a "comic song" as Sylvester Daggerwood on March 15; "Tid-re-I" and "Nature Will Prevail or a Woman" on March 16; "Tid-re-I" again on March 18; another unidentified song on March 22; "The Irish Haymaker" and "Tid-re-I" in *Harlequin's Vagaries* on March 23; and "Tid-re-I" again on March 25. On March 11, catches and glees of *The Catch Club* accompanied by Reinagle on the "pianoforte" included, in addition to "The Constitutional Glee" and "Poor Thomas Day," "The Red Cross Nights," "Here's a Health to All Good Lasses," and "O Lady Fair." On March 16 and 23 "Dr. Splash's Rambles or a Cosmetic Excursion for the Benefit of the Ladies" was sung by Jefferson; and on March 23 in Act II of *Robin Hood* "Marriage Is a Lottery or a Thousand Blanks to the Prize" by Blissett; a "new comic song" billed as having been written by the author of "The Tars of Columbia"; a "new patriotic song" sung by Hardinge on March 25, along with "The Female Auctioneer" sung by Mrs. Seymour.

The incidental dances included a hornpipe by Miss Hunt on June 25, a dance at the end of *The Temple of Flora* on June 27, a country dance in Act II of *Speed the Plough* following the popular ploughing match, and a dance by Master Harris, Miss Hunt, and Miss Scriven after *Sailors on Shore* on July 9. The trio repeated their dance on July 18. There was a hornpipe by Warrell on October 15, a **minuet** *de la cour* and a gavotte by Master Harris and Miss Hunt in Act I of *Romeo and Juliet* on January 18. In Act II of *High Life below Stairs* on January 26 there was a mock minuet by Jefferson and Mrs. Shaw. In the ballet of *The Miraculous Mill* on February 20 there was a hornpipe by Master C. Durang and an "Allemande en Trois" by Masters Harris and C. Durang and Miss Hunt. There was a dance of the fairies (composed by Francis) in Act II of *Selima and Azor* on March 6. A reel was performed by Masters Harris and Durang and Miss Hunt after *The Clandestine Marriage* on March 9. There was a "characteristic dance" in Act II of *The Sultan* on March 11, a triple hornpipe by Masters Harris and Durang and Miss Hunt in a "representation of a Neopolitan festival" in Act II of *False and True* on March 13 and, on March 20, in Act II of *The Mountaineers,* a "new Spanish fandango" composed by Francis, who appeared in it with Durang, Masters Harris and Durang and Miss Hunt. On the same night a "procession and dance" were included in Act I of *The Counterfeit.* In Scene I of *Arthur and Emmeline* on March 22 there was an Indian dance by Durang and Masters C. and F. Durang and, in Act II of *High Life below Stairs,* a mock minuet by Jefferson and Mrs. Shaw. The "Garland" dance from *A Tale of Mystery* was repeated "by desire" on March 25.

The scheduled recitations numbered only two. On June 25 the epilogue to *The Poor Gentleman* had been part of the comedy but, on January 19, "Alonzo and Imogene" was spoken by Cooper and "Giles Jallup and Brown Sally Green" by Jefferson.

The season had been unusually successful but there was to be no summer season. Yellow fever, which would take 943 lives before the year was over, may have been the reason. In any event it was a summer in which history was writing a drama of real adventure in the west. At the President's behest Lewis and Clark were exploring the territory so providentially acquired. They were to reach the Pacific in November and Zebulon Pike, who may never have ascended the Peak although he was to have it named after him, was investigating the headwaters of the Mississippi. If communications had been better and conditions more favorable to native authorship, their hazardous journeys might soon have been the inspiration for plays at the Chestnut. As it was, military and naval victories had been celebrated in some of its pieces and, in the new season, *Captain Smith and the Princess Pocahontas* was to be presented for the first time in America.

7

"Just Like Love,"

as sung by Woodham to the accompaniment of tears and sighs by the ladies.

Just like love in yonder rose,
Heavenly fragrance round it throws;
Yet tears its dewy leaves disclose,
And in the midst of briers it blows,
   Just like love.
Culled to bloom upon the breast
Since rough thorns the stems invest,
They must be gathered with the rest
   Just like love.
And when rude hands the twin buds sever,
Yet the thorn be sharp as ever—
   Just like love.

Enter the Censor
1805-1806

"MR. CENSOR," read the letter to the editor of *The Theatrical Censor*, "I was one of the immense crowd which attended the theatre on Monday evening [December 2] and was nearly squeezed to death at the box-door as I was endeavoring to carry to my wife and the little ones a pocket-full of oysters which I had procured at Mr. Vogdes' for their supper [small wonder with the curtain at 6 P.M.] and which, by the time I got in, were absolutely reduced to shrimps. So badly is this door contrived that, as not more than one can pass it at a time, it would take at least an hour for the box part of the audience to go out and return, particularly as there appeared to be a party formed to amuse themselves by obstructing the current. How easily might this be remedied by having two doors abreast, one for going out, the other for entering. A lady, who had been out to purchase a little gin, had her bottle broken, and all the precious contents ran from her pocket, in a truly odiferous shower. Another stunned us with the cry, 'I have lost my shoe'; a third had torn her shawl; and a sober, methodistical-looking gentleman solemnly declared he should *die*."

The "Censor" was the anonymous "Citizen" who, on December 9, 1805, began publication of *The Theatrical Censor,* one of the first American periodicals devoted exclusively to the stage; and the "Monday evening" was the opening night, December 2, of the Chestnut's 1805-1806 season. The *Port Folio* was still being published; but its reviews were evidently written by Dennie's friends, now that the editor, who died in 1812, was fighting a losing battle for his health and avoiding the rigors of a winter season at the Chestnut, where patrons had occasionally to stamp their feet or repair to the drinking saloons to keep themselves warm.

At first *The Theatrical Censor* must have seemed a promising venture to the theatre. But it was soon apparent that it preferred being clever and captious to being helpful. Warren and Wood had been doing their best to maintain an orderly playhouse; but the new magazine, in an article written under the pseudonym of "Dolly Dabble"—a member of its staff or a beau-about town—addressed "Mr. Sensur" in an early number claiming he was "won of the ladies hup in the hupper boxes wen the gentleman kquarrilld abowt the music, and I think itt a grate shame that they should be hallowd to make such a noize, and friten us hout of our witts. It is verry ard that wen peple goes to see the play, thay shoud be anoied by a parsel of hignorant young men who has no taste for polyte amusements." This was provocative to chronic letter-writers and it may have promoted a sensitive soul to write of the performance of *La Perouse,* on December 18, that it "would undoubtedly be more agreeable to the feminine part of the audience if less frequent use were made of firearms on the stage," albeit the flourish of a pistol was essential to the denouement of the pantomime. In a similarly capricious mood a critic masquerading as "Nicholas Botton" protested that, during the January 13 performance of *Cinderella,* a pantomime popular enough to be repeated eleven times, he "felt himself very uncomfortable on seeing several poor infants suspended by ropes, in attitudes that made him suppose that they had been placed there by punishment." Though prudes had condemned the actress playing Cinderella for changing her shoes on the stage, he seemed disappointed when Venus appeared in a blue gown trimmed with silver and wearing a "good comfortable pair of shoes and stockings." "I was a long time trying" to pick her out among the celestials, he complained; "and had it not been for the politeness of a person who sat near me and who, as often as he could desist from cracking nuts and munching apples, favored me with a word, I might have gone home without distinguishing the goddess from the nymphs."

The *Censor's* criticisms lacked the tolerance and urbanity of Dennie's. They castigated Wood for his "monotonous delivery" and "distortions of the countenance" in the role of Belcour, and Cain for "murdering" the part of Charles Dudley in *The West Indian* on December 2. Regarding Cain as Young Norval in *Douglas,* on December 18, it quoted Hamlet, "I had as lief the town-crier spoke my lines." In *The Road to Ruin* on December 13 it condemned Mrs. Wood's "unnatural laugh" as Sophia; and it suggested Blissett, who played Silky, "might be more happy in his drunken scene were he to study the graces," adding that, "strange as it may appear, there is a grace to be observed even in drunkenness." Of Rutherford as Davidson in *Mary, Queen of Scots* on January 15, it asserted that he "takes more pains with his feet than with his head" and "always appears to be preparing for a minuet." There were two performers with whom the *Censor* had a special crow to pick. One was Taylor whose "appearance and manner" as Rowley in *The School for Scandal* on December 11, the *Censor* claims, were "like those of a London undertaker soliciting a job." The other was the brilliant Jefferson whose "constant swinging and twisting of the body," as Solomon Gundy in *Who Wants a Guinea?* on December 26 "must be offensive to every eye," thought the Censor, "and only becomes the stage of the charlatan." After Jefferson's appearance as Will Steady in *The Purse or the Benevolent Tar,* on January 27, the magazine even versified its objection.

> Ah! Jefferson, why so much wit would you make
> To consist, my dear lad, in a wiggle and shake?
> Away with the trick, and your vein, never doubt it,
> Would flow through the scene just as comic without it;
> But if, fond of shaking, at precepts you scoff,
> Shake a good shake at once, man! and shake the thing off.

But there were highly favorable criticisms, too. Of Mrs. Melmoth from the New York theatre, who made her Philadelphia debut as Lady St. Valori in *The Carmelite,* the *Censor* reported that her voice was melodious, her gesticulation dignified, and her countenance expressive. Jefferson shone as a "good low comedian" in the role of Jeremy Diddler in *Raising the Wind.* While condemning Mrs. Woodham, making her bow on December 6, for wearing, as Little Pickle in *The Spoiled Child,* "that appendage to manhood, vulgarly yclep'd breeches," the *Censor* admitted that she added to her good figure "the graces of action peculiar to her sex." It pronounced Bray, a newcomer from the New York and Leeds theatres, "a young man of much promise." On the same night of December 11 Mrs. Wignell was "excellent as Lady Teazle." On December 18, Jefferson as the monkey (a role in which his fidgets were appropriate), and Blissett as the valet of Perouse, the Censor objectively reported, "were applauded to the skies." Mrs. Cunningham from the Edinburgh theatre gave "general satisfaction" as Lucretia MacTab in *The Poor Gentleman* on December 20.

On January 2 Wood's performance of Dick Dowlas in *The Heir at Law*, the *Censor* admitted, "was superior to anything we have before seen of that gentleman's efforts. He personified admirably the awkward gait of a freshly made beau; and, by constant grinning, peeping through his glass, playing with his watch-chain, and flourishing every moment an enormous white handkerchief, marked the difference between the well-bred man and a mushroom buck."

The *Censor* also praised Reinagle "for the arrangement of music between the scenes of [*Mary, Queen of Scots*, on January 15]. It was a fine treat to those who are pleased with Scotch ballads." Pleading for a greater appreciation of the composer's efforts, the *Censor* added: "The Hottentots in the gallery, however, were bawling for Tid-re-I and Jefferson's March. Would these gentlemen were marched off in the time of the former tune! The constables, we conceive, would be more advantageously employed in this boisterous region than at the doors. The talisman of these gentlemen might be sometimes well applied to the throats of the lovers of Tid-re-I."

Contributions to the *Port Folio* were supplementing the *Censor's* criticisms now and then. On January 20, though Wood and Mrs. Woodham were disappointing, Fennell played an animated Zanga in *The Revenge*; and, in the afterpiece, though McKenzie was too British and too tame as the whimsical Scotsman, Sir Archy, Harwood was "good" as the "Hibernian jontleman," Sir Callahan. The *Port Folio* praised Fennell as Glenalvon and Mrs. Melmoth as Lady Randolph in *Douglas,* on February 1; but it could be caustic when necessary. Cain as Young Norval sank "beneath the weight of his burden." Wood's Iago on February 3 was "not villainous enough." On the same night it was an insult to the public that the "little bundle-breeched figure" of Miss Hunt in *The Shipwreck* was made to compensate for the omission of songs. Fennell, however, deserved his full house as Othello (after seeing him in it a Southern planter once offered to buy him), though the *Port Folio* critic felt he could play it with "more fire," maintaining that, if Fennell were "less a scholar he could be a greater actor. He would have shone more at the bar or in the pulpit than on the stage." Mrs. Wignell and Mrs. Melmoth "displayed their usual attractions" as Desdemona and Emilia.

The *Censor* agreed that Fennell was "good" as the Moor. Engagements with Fennell and Cooper were making possible the performance of eight of Shakespeare's plays. Effective as ever, Cooper, playing Macbeth on March 17, "had the honor of drawing tears from more than one of the Indian chiefs who were present" as they sat in their hybrid costumes of rough coats and mocassins, their faces smeared with coarse ochre and with copper or silver ornaments dangling from their ears. The scholarly Harwood had returned after a six-year absence and the *Censor* approves of the $900 he received at his benefit, agreeing with the public that "as a performer, in many characters, he is very great." Of Cross, from Edinburgh, recruited in Britain by Warren like Mrs. Woodham, Bray, and Mrs. Cunningham, the *Censor* admits that his part of Major O'Flaherty in *The West Indian,* on December 2, while "badly performed" was "well conceived"; and it might have paid tribute to his good singing voice and his invaluable assistance in staging the pantomimes. It might also have pointed out that the handsome, genteel-looking Woodham, making his début three nights after his wife's on December 9, as Paul in *Paul and Virginia,* made up for his limited acting ability by being an excellent singer and tenor solo trumpet performer.

With only exhibitions of wild animals and occasional Southwark performances of Manfredi and his three daughters on the tight rope and in petite pantomimes to compete with them, the acting managers, Warren and Wood, strove to justify their monopoly with thirteen new pieces, five for the first time in America; and the artists, with their thick coating of color, whiting, and glue (eliminating glare from the lamps and the inflammability of oil), doubled their efforts to produce attractive settings for the dramas and pantomimes. Their *pièce de résistance* was the scenery for *Cinderella,* produced for the first time in America on January 1. "The clouds in which Hymen and the cupids ascend and descend," approved the *Censor,* "have a very fine effect, bestowing unqualified praise on the talents of the painter." Byrne's version of this story, whose ramifications are legion in the literatures of the world, was an importation from Drury Lane, where it had been "performed upwards of 100 nights," declared an advertisement, "to overflowing houses." With its glimpses of the "Prince's Palace," "Cinderella's Kitchen," a "splendid Ballroom," the appeal its theme always has to the imagination of childhood, and its illusive changes (including the transformation of the mice into horses), the pantomime drew so many children to the Chestnut that on January 13 it was presented as an opening piece so the tots could be tucked into bed at a decent hour. *The Brazen Mask,* given its American première on March 1 and by Fawcett, the author of *Three-Fingered Jack* and *La Perouse,* was another artistic triumph for Holland, Robbins, and H. Reinagle. But the artists' most ambitious canvas was a 924 square-foot representation of "The Battle of Derne," designed and painted by Holland, Smith, and H. Reinagle. Displayed for the first time on March 14, it showed Eaton and O'Bannon in action, the *Argus* brig, *Nautilus* schooner and *Hornet* sloop in the bay and, on their starboard, the fort which O'Bannon captured.

> Such scenes tonight with patriot warmth portrayed,
> To grace our stage the painter has displayed

ran a part of the lines written for the occasion,

> Here to your eyes the zealous artist shows
> How toiled your heroes and how fell your foes,

How generous Eaton in his country's might
For You and Freedom dared the mortal fight,
Shows how O'Bannon, the brave among the brave,
Taught Moors to dread the White Men of the wave.
Undaunted Spence! for thee the colours flow;
For thee Decatur, still they warmer glow.

There followed a new song composed by C. Harford and sung by Woodham, a song by Robbins written for the occasion and a characteristic dance composed by Francis with an "allegorical transparency" entitled "American Heroes or Decatur, Preble and Eaton."

By the season of 1805-1806 music had become an almost obtrusive part of the bills. On March 3 after *Romeo and Juliet* there was a concerto on the violin by Gillingham, and on March 5 a trumpet and bugle horn obligato by Woodham. On March 12 a concert of vocal and instrumental "musick" included "Within These Shady Bowers" sung by Robbins; a comic song sung by Jefferson; "The Soldier Tired of War's Alarms" with an accompaniment by Woodham on the trumpet, sung by Mrs. Seymour; a "concertante" with the "pianoforte" and harp, by Woodham and DeBreuys; a glee, "When Sappho Tuned," by Robbins, Woodham, and Gillingham; and, "by desire," the overture of *The Battle of Prague,* with a trumpet and bugle horn obligato by Woodham and an "augmented" band under Gillingham. In Act I of *Don Juan,* on March 26, Robbins, Woodham, and Mrs. Seymour as serenaders sang Moore's glee of "Oh Lady Fair"; and Jefferson, as Scaramouch, "See That Pretty Creature There." Robbins, as a sailor, sang "Come, Jolly Boys, Let's Sailors Be"; and Mrs. Seymour, "Thus for Men the Women Fare."

The incidental songs were Dibdin's "Flowing Can," by Mrs. Woodham, December 6; a duet, as Genevieve and Claudine in *The Hunter of the Alps,* by Mrs. Seymour and Miss Hunt, December 11; "Just Like Love," by Woodham,

Enter the Censor 83

December 20, January 29, in *Paul and Virginia* March 28; "Gentle Cousin John," by Mrs. Wignell, in *The Sailor's Daughter,* January 8; a "favorite song" at the end of Act IV of *The Way to Get Married,* sung by Woodham, January 10, when there was a "new medley overture" composed by Mr. Taylor of Philadelphia; "The Galley Slave," by Woodham in *The Purse,* on January 27; an epithalamium in Act III of *Isabella,* February 14; in *The Farmer,* "Bonny Bet" by Woodham and "The Ploughboy" by Francis, February 19; after *The Blind Bargain,* "The Cosmetic Doctor" and "Knowing Joe" by Jefferson, "Murder in Irish" by Harwood, a song by Woodham, February 26; a "favorite song" by Woodham after *Pizarro,* February 28; a dirge by the characters in *Romeo and Juliet,* Act V, March 3; after *John Bull,* "William Tell" by Woodham, who also played the overture to *The Battle of Prague,* also a comic song by Harwood, March 5; the glee of "The Red Cross Knights," March 7; "Tid-re-I," by Jefferson and, after an interlude from *The Critic,* a new song by Harwood, sung by Robbins to Woodham's trumpet accompaniment, March 10; the dancing duet of "Tink-a-Tink" by Harwood as Shacabac and Mrs. Woodham as Beda in an interlude from *Bluebeard,* March 12; and a song as Juliana by Mrs. Wignell, in *The Honeymoon,* March 15, April 2 and 7.

There was the usual complement of dancing, in which the children of the theatre (Master Harris, three of the young Durangs, and two of Jefferson's children) played an important part. On December 2 in the last scene of *The May-Day Dower,* there was a reel by Masters Harris and Durang and Miss Hunt. On December 24 and February 7 the children performed a dance, *The Sailor's Return from Tripoli,* founded on *The Sailor's Landlady,* in which, says the Censor, their "pantomimical powers" were "extremely amusing," and proof of the industry of their teachers, Francis and Durang. In *The Sailor's Return from Tripoli,* on December

24 and February 7 there were a triple hornpipe by Masters Harris and Durang and Miss Hunt, a fling by Masters Jefferson and A. Durang, and a reel by the characters. In Scene II of *Paul and Virginia* on December 9, January 29, and March 28 there was a "characteristic dance" by Masters Harris, Durang, and Jefferson. Other dances included a mock minuet in Act II of *High Life below Stairs* by Jefferson and Mrs. Woodham on December 27; a country dance to accompany the inevitable "ploughing match" in Act II of *Speed the Plough* on January 3; a new country dance composed by Francis in Act IV of *The Honeymoon* on February 24, March 15, April 2 and 7; a "characteristic dance" in Act I of *Romeo and Juliet* by Masters Harris and Durang and Miss Hunt; and a Scotch hornpipe at the end of *John Bull* which Mrs. Woodham danced on March 5.

As for scheduled recitations, there was the epilogue to *The Carmelite,* spoken by Mrs. Melmoth on December 4, and "Dryden's Ode," after *The Blind Bargain* on February 26 by Mrs. Melmoth; "Dennis Brulgruddery's Description of Pizarro," on February 28, and after *Pizarro* "The Birth, Christening, Marriage and Other Family Misfortunes of Dennis Brulgruddery" on March 12, both by Harwood; and at the end of *Lewis of Monteblanco* on March 10 an address written by Harwood and spoken by Wood and Harwood as the Prince of Wales and Sir John Falstaff. There was another, previous to *The Voice of Nature,* the most effective of these addresses, given on January 31 by the orphan children of Hodgkinson, who had died of yellow fever in Washington the previous summer. "A full house," reports the *Censor,* "cheered the hearts of the little orphans, who exerted themselves to express their gratitude" on the occasion, which was for their benefit; and Miss F. Hodgkinson danced *La Chantreuse,* as taught her by M. Lalliet.

In the season, which closed April 9, 1806, Mrs. Wignell was still a "wonderfully tender and impressive" Ophelia, in the opinion of the *Censor*. Wood, too, held his own against competition and Warren was as captivating a Sir John as ever, while Fennell, the old favorite, was adding to the prestige of the company by reading Shakespeare to the non-theatregoing Quakers at the University of Pennsylvania. Two American plays, *Captain Smith and the Princess Pocahontas* and *The Fox Chase,* its prologue spoken by McKenzie, were among the new offerings; and, in the following season, as proof of the progressive spirit of the managers, who had at their disposal a wealth of English material and the actors to interpret it, there were to be as many as three original American plays.

8

Patriotism and Pantomime
1806-1807

VICTORY OVER the Barbary pirates and the storms and stresses that culminated in the Embargo Act of December 22, 1807 were testing the ship of state and proving it seaworthy. On Independence Day, 1806, the front of the Chestnut Street Theatre, in keeping with the spirit of the occasion was "ornamented with a grand transparency," in a season running from June 18 to July 9. After the comedy of *He Would Be a Soldier,* "Jefferson's March" by Reinagle was played and a "Eulogium on the American Worthies" recited by Mrs. Melmoth. There was a song by Mrs. Poe of the Virginia theatre who, in less than three years, was to become the mother of the literary genius bearing her name; and there was "The Yorkshire Irishman or the Adventures of a Potato Merchant," sung by Bray. Mrs. Seymour returned to the martial note with "A Soldier Tired of War's Alarms" and Mrs. Melmoth recited "The Blackbirds." Jefferson offered a comic and Mrs. Poe a sentimental relief in their respective songs of "Giles Scroggins' Ghost" and "He Stole My Heart Away." But the bill was chiefly patriotic with its finale of a panorama of "The Battle of Tripoli," as painted by Holland, the song, "A Soldier is the Noblest Name," sung by Robbins, and a characteristic dance composed by Francis, with an allegorical transparency called "The American Heroes or Decatur, Preble and Eaton," and a transparent painting representing "Liberty, Columbia and Justice."

During the brief summer session, most of the other songs were comic or sentimental: a comic number by Jefferson on June 23, together with "The Bay of Biscay," a new one sung by Robbins, "The Adventures of a Yorkshire Potatoe Merchant," sung by Bray, and on June 30, "Grizzle and Pigs," sung as Sylvester Daggerwood by Jefferson. On the same date Mrs. Poe, as Biddy Bellair in *Miss in Her Teens*, reverted to the martial "A Bonny Bold Soldier."

It echoed the sentiment on the other side of the lamps though the Chestnut's managers were more immediately concerned with the battles within the theatre. With their excellent company and the patronage it enjoyed, they were in the favored position of being able to attract the most promising players on either side of the Atlantic. On June 20 Mrs. Poe had reappeared at the Chestnut as Rosina, after an absence of five years; and though her husband, who bowed to Philadelphia on the same date as Young Norval, was ineffective, a "young gentleman" later identified as Cone, who "made his first appearance on any stage" as Achmet in *Barbarossa* on June 27, became a valuable player and, for the fall season opening December 1, 1806, the managers also acquired Mr. and Mrs. Mills of the Manchester theatre and a "musical phenomenon"—to quote the *Port Folio*— from the Dublin stage, a tenor named Webster, who won instant acclaim as Young Meadows, on December 17, both for the sweetness and power of his voice and for his acting.

But the assemblage of such talent created a problem for the managers, who had to deal with the jealousies and dissatisfactions of the Green Room. Harwood had withdrawn from the company when he had been unable to secure the parts which other players refused to relinquish and the temperamental squabbles were weighing heavily on the fifty-year old Reinagle, busy as he was with his composing and directing, and to such a degree on the Widow Wignell, now thirty-seven and retiring by nature, that she placed her heart and her share of the business at the disposal of Warren, whom she married on August 15, 1806.

This was the first step toward a fortunate partnership between Warren and Wood which was to last until 1826, and it was immediately reflected in improvements on the outside and inside of the theatre building and in the quality and arrangement of the bills presented. On January 23 and 30, as much for its nautical flavor, currently popular, as for the dancing ability of the theatre's children, *The Sailor's Return from Tripoli* was repeated, with its triple hornpipe by Masters Harris and Durang and Miss Hunt, its fling by Masters Jefferson and A. Durang, and its reel by the entire cast. It was under the direction, as previously, of Francis and John Durang, whose remarkable family of three boys and five girls included Ferdinand, said to be the first to sing "The Star-Spangled Banner" in public, in a building adjoining the Holliday Street Theatre in Baltimore, with his brother Charles leading the chorus. Charles himself, one of the little garrison who guarded the six-gun battery at the battle of North Point, Md., later became an actor, ballet master, manager, and stage historian.

More specifically patriotic was the bill of February 23, which, in honor of Washington's birthday, included an "emblematical transparency and the apotheosis of that lamented hero," followed by a characteristic dance by Masters Harris, Durang, F. Durang, A. Durang, Cunningham, and Jefferson,

and the Misses Hunt, Mullen, and Scriven. The transparency
was shown again and the apotheosis repeated on March 25,
when Robbins sang a new patriotic song written by C. Harford, with music by Bray, called "The Glory of Columbia,
Her Yeomanry," accompanied on the trumpet by Woodham
and followed by a characteristic dance.

On April 11, after *Love Makes a Man,* there was a "grand
spectacle" called "Miscellaneous Ball or The Carnival
Masquerade of Venice," in which was shown an allegorical
transparency designed and executed by Holland and Robbins, entitled "American Heroes or The Naval Garland" in
honor of the officers who fell in the engagement off Tripoli.
The transparency, shown again on April 13, pictured the
Goddess of America on the right, Commodore Preble, lifesize, on the left, the frigate *Constitution* in the background
and, "in the sky part," the busts of Captain Decatur, Summers, Wadsworth, Caldwell, Israel, and Dorsey. The
Durangs, who were receiving a benefit on April 11, displayed their versatility. In addition to playing Tom Thumb,
Master A. Durang sang "Giles Scroggins' Ghost." Master
C. Durang danced a *minuet de la cour* and *pas russe* with
Miss Hunt, and Master F. Durang a hornpipe. Their father
performed some feats of "Herculean agility and free vaulting" on the slack rope, with Barnett acting as the clown.
Mrs. Woodham danced a "Scottish allegorical *pas seul*" and
there was a garland dance by the characters (the play not
specified), followed by a "display of a superb transparency
imitating chrystal, lately the property of Signior Belogno,
who exhibited them [*sic*] at Covent Garden with universal
applause, called the Brilliances of Perrico."

On April 13, the artists again displayed their "Battle of
Derne," "The Blowing Up of a Gunboat," and "The Battle
of Tripoli," and a new transparency in honor of Captain
Decatur, another of an "Eagle bearing the resolution of
Congress expressive of its sense of Bravery" [*sic*] and an-

other of Captain Preble (taken from the gold medal presented to him by Congress), as painted by J. B. Smith.

In mapping out the season the Chestnut's managers also bore in mind their public's taste for music, scenery, and romantic story, as combined in the pantomimes and the new genre of the "melodrame." *Cinderella* and *La Perouse* were repeated and three new melodrames presented, *Valentine and Orson* as many as seven times. The last proved more fetching than even the farce of *The Weathercock,* with its protean hero, Tristram Fickle, entrancingly played by Jefferson. Reinagle contributed some original music to the pantomime; the artists some attractive views of the city of Orleans, a convent garden, the interior of a king's palace, and "the Forest of Orleans," with its menace of wild animals (which Philadelphians were eager to see whenever they were "exposed" in the town). The plot of *Valentine and Orson* was such as would appeal to an audience childishly fond of simple fables—about a hero vowing to deliver his country from a monster in the guise of a Wild Man of the Woods.

For their patrons with more cultivated tastes the managers presented a dozen of Shakespeare's plays, with the aging and unhappy Fennell carrying the burden of the heavier masculine roles, now that Cooper had become manager of the Park. Mrs. Warren ran through her usual repertory and the beautiful but towering Mrs. Melmoth appeared appropriately as the dominating Lady Macbeth, and as Queen Catherine opposite Warren as Henry VIII. With his expanding girth, Warren could be made to look more and more like the Holbein portrait of the much-marrying monarch. He also re-created his Falstaff for both parts of *Henry IV* and *The Merry Wives.*

With their duties so ably discharged, Warren and Wood, now managers in more than name, had little to fear from the remarks of *The Theatrical Censor and Critical Miscellany* which, with its enlarged title, began publication on Septem-

Patriotism and Pantomime 91

ber 27. Some of them were barbed. Cone's "enunciation and tragedy airs," as Frederick in *Lovers' Vows* on December 3, were "laughable." Wood might have "unbent more" as Anhalt and Warren been less "boisterous" as the Baron. Bray and Mrs. Francis as the Cottager and his wife "overstepped in bowing"—doubtless a Republican sentiment. Mills as Robert Tyke in *The School of Reform,* on December 5, was "excellent till he became tragic in the part," then he "excited laughter." His sister, Mrs. Woodham, as Julia, affected "too much an infantile manner." But the *Censor* was enthusiastic about some of the other performances and a number of its criticisms (such as Francis' using too many gestures) were matters of personal opinion. *Chacun à son goût!*

As for taste, there was variety enough in the bills of 1806-1807 to suit everybody. Seventeen pieces were presented in the summer and 136 in the regular season, including 37 comedies, 23 tragedies, 12 comic operas and 12 farces, a repertory exceeding any of a modern era. In the season ending April 23, 1807, there were 6 comedies, 1 farce, 3 musical farces, 2 historical dramas, 3 melodramas, and 2 "musical entertainments" offered for the first time in Philadelphia; and, for the first time in America, 2 comedies, 1 farce, and 3 musical pieces. Three of the six were American: *Peeping Tom of Coventry,* by a "young gentleman" of Philadelphia, billed as "not acted these 8 years" but probably never before played; *Tears and Smiles,* with its prologue spoken by Wood and lyrical epilogue sung by Jefferson; and *The Generous Farmers,* preceded by an occasional address spoken by its author, Mrs. Melmoth.

With Webster added to the staff of singers, the songs were numerous and varied. *The Sons of Apollo,* an interlude on March 11, over which Francis presided as president, Mills as senior vice president and Cain as junior vice president, mustered Warren, Robbins, Gillingham, Webster, Bray, and Gross as "harmonics," and Webster to sing "Down in the Valley," which he repeated on March 14. Webster, Gillingham, Robbins, Jefferson, and Bray sang the glees of "Glorious Apollo" and "My Mother Had a Maid Called Barbara." Jefferson repeated his comic song, "Giles Scroggins' Ghost," and the interlude ended with the glee of "Red Cross Knights," accompanied like the other glees and songs by Woodham on the pianoforte. When *The Sons of Apollo* was repeated on March 14, "Sigh no More Ladies" and "Here's a Health to All Good Lasses" were substituted for the glees of "My Mother, etc." and "Red Cross Knights."

One of the most popular of the incidental songs was "At the Front of the Cottage," as sung with engaging simplicity by Mrs. Warren in the role of Juliana in *The Honeymoon* on December 8, 29, January 21, and February 14. Another favorite was "Tell Her I Love Her," as sung by Webster in the role of Young Meadows, on December 17, after *Speed the Plough* on December 26, and after *Pizarro* on January 7. Another was "Giles Scroggins' Ghost," as sung by Jefferson on March 21 and April 4 and by Master A. Durang at the family's benefit on April 11. Applauded, too, was "The Thorn," also sung by Webster on December 17. The season's other songs and musical numbers, some of them equally popular, had a sentimental trend. There was the song of "The Love Letter," which Woodham sang as Robin Hood, and of "The Rose," composed by the versatile Bray, which Webster sang as Edwin on December 22. There was the "celebrated" duet of "All's Well," sung by Woodham and Webster at the end of Act II of *Speed the Plough* on December 26, and on January 9 the "Bird Song" from the opera *The Cabinet,* sung by Webster as Signior in *The Son-in-Law.* A song by Jefferson as Sylvester Daggerwood on January 14 and again on April 1 offered comedy relief; and, after a solemn dirge concluding *Romeo and Juliet* on February 6, Webster returned to the romantic vein with his song of "The Thorn." On February 27 Gillingham played a concerto on the violin.

After a dead march for Coriolanus on March 16 Webster as Paudeen O'Rougherty sang "Kate Karney" and Mrs. Melmoth as Mrs. Manley sang "Drimindoo" in *The Generous Farmers*. Two nights later, Webster, as Carlos, sang an additional song, "The Maid of Lodi," and Mrs. Melmoth, as the Duenna, sang additional songs. There was an epithalamium at the end of *Isabella* on March 21 and a musical entertainment called *Olla Podrida* consisting of "The Yorkshire Irishman" sung by Bray, and "Tid-re-I" by Webster, in addition to Jefferson's "Ghost" song. On March 23 "Madame Fig's Gala" was sung by Bray as Dennis Moorpont, and Webster sang "My Sweet Molly Mog" as Paddy O'Carrol in *Donald Mackintosh's Travels,* an interlude taken from *The Register Office*. On March 28 "The Storm" and "Black-Eyed Susan" and on April 3, after *The Busybody,* a new trumpet song composed by the Philadelphian C. Harford with the words by Bray were sung by Webster, the last to an accompaniment by Woodham. To *Melocosmiotes,* on April 4, Bray contributed "The Yorkshire Irishman," which he repeated after *The Clandestine Marriage* on April 15. After *The Battle of Hexham,* on April 8, he sang the comic song of "The Lord Mayor's Shew" and "Mrs. Bond" as Jerry Sneak in *The Mayor of Garrat*.

In Act II of the historical drama there were the glees, "When Arthur First at Court Began" and "Lurk, Lurk O'er the Green Sward" and, after the farce, a new song by C. Harford and Bray, accompanied on the trumpet by Woodham. After *The Distressed Mother,* on April 10, Jefferson sang "Knowing Joe"; and, after *The Clandestine Marriage* on April 15 "The Cosmetic Doctor." After *The Way to Get Married,* on April 18, Woodham sang "Just Like Love," F. Durang "The Yorkshire Irishman," and Jefferson repeated "Knowing Joe." The finale and chorus of *The Travellers,* on April 20, were "set" by Reinagle.

The dancing was keeping step with the music. Miss Hunt had profited from the tutelage of Francis, one of the best ballet masters in the country, and been praised by the *Censor* a number of times. In the 1806-1807 season she appeared in a characteristic dance, a part of the Country Fair in Act II of *Marian,* on January 30; together with Masters Harris and Durang in another characteristic dance, part of a Masquerade in Act I of *Romeo and Juliet,* on February 6; with other juveniles in still another characteristic dance concluding *Love and Money,* on March 18; again with the same juveniles and Master Cunningham in an Irish Lilt, after *The Two Misers,* on March 20; in *The Irish Haymakers,* part of *Olla Podrida,* on March 21; and in a solo hornpipe in *Melocosmiotes* on April 4. Favorites among the adults were Mills and Mrs. Woodham, whose "tall, symmetrical figure, animated features and graceful attitudes," in the descriptive language of the historian Durang, enhanced the effect of their Scots dance on February 2, their highland reel and fling on March 18, their strathspey concluding *The Gentle Shepherd* on March 26, and their highland reel after *The Distressed Mother* on April 10. In *The Rival Sisters,* on April 3, Mrs. Woodham danced a hornpipe. Other dances were a country dance by the characters at the end of Act IV of *The Honeymoon* on December 8 and January 21; a "statue" scene and dance by the characters in Act I of *Love in a Village* on December 17 and February 16; the country dance by the characters accompanying the ploughing match in *Speed the Plough* on December 26; an Irish jig by the characters and Masters Harris, Durang, F. and A. Durang, and Miss Scriven concluding *The Generous Farmers* on March 16; and a characteristic dance composed by Francis, performed on April 13 before the allegorical transparency called "American Heroes Or Decatur, Preble and Eaton."

There were a few recitations during the season. Fennell, whose declamatory style had become a little outmoded, was still effective in the "Friends, Romans, Countrymen" scene of Mark Antony, whom he impersonated after *Romeo and Juliet* on February 6, against the background of the Roman Forum. There was an occasional address delivered by Cain, previous to *Tancred and Sigismunda* on March 14; and another by Webster after *The Cabinet* on March 28 (hardly to be listed as recitations at all), and Dryden's "Ode of Alexander's Feast" spoken by Cone at his benefit on April 10.

There was what might be termed a special event after *The Poor Gentleman* on April 6. It was billed as "The Dwarf Dance or The Whimsical Transformation from a dwarf of three feet to a woman six feet high," an histrionic miracle that will have to remain obscured by the mists of time. There followed a duet by Robbins and Woodham, "Freedom on Thy Fertile Plains," and "Dr. Goldsmith's Epilogue," delivered by Mills with a leap through a barrel of fire seven feet high, something more in the nature of a Southwark performance.

Unusual, too, was an event occurring on April 15, a week before the season ended. It was a benefit for Lewis Hallam, so closely identified with American theatrical history. He appeared as Lord Ogleby in *The Clandestine Marriage* on the occasion of the fifty-sixth year of his appearance on the Philadelphia stage. The occasion was theatrically historical, as it was the first time he ever acted at the Chestnut.

9

Audience Reaction: The Embargo 1807-1808

"A CIRCUMSTANCE occurred in the theatre on Saturday evening last, [March 26, 1808] which displayed a very high degree of turpitude." An article in the *American Daily Advertiser* continues, "Some person in one of the upper boxes threw a lighted squib into the pit, which fell among a circle of decently dressed women, and terrified them excessively. They were, however, fortunate enough to extinguish it without suffering any serious injury. As the wicked deed was perpetrated in a moment, and the squib instantaneously extinguished, the miscreant escaped the punishment due to guilt, very few of the audience being aware of the real nature of the occurrence which excited the alarm. A few nights before, some villain threw a knife upon the stage, apparently, with a design to wound a reputable actress, then on the boards, who narrowly escaped from the intended injury."

The knife-thrower may have been a son of Neptune out

of employment as a result of the Embargo Act, signed by President Jefferson on December 22, 1807. On June 22, as a climax to the high-handed actions of the British on the seas, the *Leopard*, one of their ships, had fired on the American frigate *Chesapeake*, and taken off four of her sailors, three of them American. Feeling against the British had reached so high a pitch that, on March 9, 1808, when Henry V declared "I thought upon one pair of English legs did march three Frenchmen," there ensued a riot that threatened to bring the performance to an end. The times were out of joint for the managers and America's melting pot was beginning to boil over at unpredictable moments. When Webster, the Dublin tenor, accused of a morals offense, was "hissed and pelted off the stage" of the Chestnut, the Irish in Philadelphia took up his cause. The rioters tore down glass chandeliers and threw them at Webster, but his friends retaliated by blackening eyes and bloodying noses in the upper saloons and lobbies of the theatre and in the streets and at least three hundred of them carried him home in triumph to his lodgings in George Street. The onus fell heavily on Barker, the Philadelphia author of *The Indian Princess,* the first Indian play by an American as presented on April 6, 1808, when the presence of Webster, in the role of Larry, the Irishman, was the cause of a demonstration that brought down the curtain, in Durang's words, "on rude commotion."

But Warren and Wood, though English and Canadian by birth, were imbued with a sentiment that prompted them, without regard to public demand, to ornament the front of the theatre, on July 4, 1807, with an emblematical transparent painting representing "Liberty, Columbia and Justice." After *Town and Country,* on December 26, they introduced an entertainment of singing, dancing, and recitation called *The Spirit of Independence,* in which they exhibited a Grand Emblematical Transparency of "The Genius of

America," designed and executed by Robbins. Shown again on January 1, 1808, it contained 180 square feet of canvas. In its center was the Genius of Liberty, environed by a portico of her temple, holding the bust of the President of the United States beneath the American Eagle, supporting the Arms of the Union with Ancient and Modern Trophies of War. On the right she was supported by the Goddess of Wisdom, bearing the spear and shield, on the left by Justice, with her balance. On January 1 the transparency ascended and, at the same time, pillars arose from a Sea of Fire, forming the whole stage into The Temple of Freedom. The advertisement explains that the figures in the transparency were seven feet high.

Appropriately Mrs. Seymour sang "The Bonny Bold Soldier" and Mrs. Melmoth recited a "Eulogium on the American Worthies." Francis, Durang, Masters Harris and Durang, and the Misses Hunt and Mullen danced a martial cotillion. Accompanied on the trumpet, Robbins sang "The Standard of Freedom," written by the actor Mills and composed by John Cole of Baltimore. There was a hornpipe by Miss Hunt and a song by Webster. There followed a *pas seul "en militaire,"* by Master F. Durang, and a song, "The Host That Fight for Liberty," by Mrs. Mills, the words by her husband, the music by Mineckey; also a song "in the character of a female volunteer." Ending the bill was a characteristic country dance called "The United Volunteers," as interpreted by Francis, Durang, Masters Harris, C. and F. Durang, Cunningham, Mrs. Durang, and the Misses Hunt and Mullen.

The managers again struck a patriotic note on January 8, with a "martial cotillion" in a masquerade in Act I of *Romeo and Juliet* by Masters Harris and Durang and Miss Hunt, and the display of a transparency at the end of *Adrian and Orilla* on Washington's birthday, and an apotheosis of the "late commander-in-chief." On March 16 they produced *The*

Audience Reaction: The Embargo

Embargo, by Barker, expressing resentment over the highhanded actions of both the French and the English; and on March 18 *The Anniversary of Shelah,* an entertainment of scenery, songs, and dancing in which native views were displayed, the song of "The Standard of Freedom," was repeated by Robbins, and the "Liberty, Wisdom and Justice" transparency was again exhibited.

Most of the bills were devised with an eye to their effect as a whole. On March 23 The Shakespeare Jubilee, repeated in a season offering eleven Shakespeare plays, included the "Jubilee Song," "The Warwickshire Thief," sung by Blissett and Francis, "The Mulberry Tree," by Robbins, Francis, and Cross, "Sweet Willy O," sung by Mrs. Seymour, "All This for a Poet," sung by Miss Hunt; and, in Act II, a pageant of most of the prominent characters of Shakespeaker's plays, its last scene displaying a bust of the Bard supported by the Tragic and the Comic muse and concluding with a roundelay and chorus.

On March 28 came "The Catch Club," with Mills acting as President and Rutherford and Cone Senior and Junior Vice President. Robbins, Webster, Gillingham, Blissett, Bray, Francis, and Cross were the Harmonics. The bill included the glee, "Sigh No More, Ladies," by Webster, Gillingham, Jefferson, and Robbins; "Faithless Emma," sung by Webster; "Giles Scroggins' Ghost," sung by Jefferson; the catch, " 'Twas You, Sir," by Francis, Blissett, Jefferson, and Robbins; "The Glasses Sparkle on the Board," which Webster was requested to sing; and the glee, "Here's a Health to All Good Lasses." The song and glees were accompanied on the pianoforte by Taylor.

At a benefit for his sons and himself, on April 9, Durang presented Master F. Durang in a hornpipe at the end of *Adrian and Orilla* and Master A. Durang in the song of "Giles Scroggins' Ghost," as a prelude to *Tom Thumb* the Great. After the pantomime he offered a spectacle called

Phantasmagori. It was a "display of optical illusions which introduces the phantoms or apparitions of the dead or absent, in a way more completely illusive than has ever yet been witnessed. This Spectrology," continues the advertisement, "professes to expose and open the eyes of those who still foster an absurd belief in ghosts. The public are respectfully informed that Mr. Durang has reserved this entire new species of entertainment for this occasion. Purchased of Sig. Bologno of Covent Garden Theatre, who has performed them at the theatres in London, Bath and Paris with universal applause."

Durang had already tried his hand at producing. After a summer season at the Chestnut, running from June 22 to July 10, 1807, he had opened the Southwark on September 22 for a season closing October 12, on his benefit night flying "from the gallery to the stage"—the date and means a matter of conjecture and bringing in $350, an impressive sum for the old theatre.

Durang, of course, had been schooled by managers who planned their seasons as carefully as their individual bills. In their Summer period they had produced 17 pieces, among them *To Marry or Not to Marry,* new to Philadelphians. In the fall, among their 130 pieces were 39 comedies, 21 farces, 16 tragedies, 11 comic operas, with 11 of the total new to Philadelphia and four of them never as yet produced in America. Yet their schedule was flexible enough for the managers to repeat the plays that proved popular, *Town and Country, Adrian and Orilla* (both new this season to Philadelphia), and *The Fortress,* presented at the Chestnut for the first time in America on February 26, with views of a "hall in the Fortress of Guntzbourg," the "interior of a Castle Yard," including a dungeon, guard room, and porter's lodge, and a *"place d'armes."* For this "melodrame," Robbins, assisted by Stuart, designed and painted new scenery.

As for the company there were no additions of importance.

Audience Reaction: The Embargo

The petite Mrs. Wilmot, formerly Mrs. Marshall, with her round face, sparkling eyes, and arch and sprightly expression, appeared as Peggy in *The Country Girl* and *Rosina* on June 24, 1807, after an absence of eight years. Two nights later Wilmot bowed as David and his wife played Julie in *The Rivals.*

On September 26, in the Southwark season, Mrs. Barrett, after a four-year absence, used her stately figure and bland countenance to advantage in acting Lady Randolph in *Douglas,* with Barrett in the role of Old Norval and their thirteen-year-old son, billed as the Infant American Roscius, in the role of Young Norval, one of his stepping-stones to a distinguished career as a genteel comedian. Serson of the Boston theatre, a negligible actor who also gave readings, appeared for the first time in Philadelphia, on January 2, as Trueman in *George Barnwell.* More notable, however, was the return of Bernard who, after an absence of five years, played Ogleby in *The Clandestine Marriage;* and the regular players were adding to their laurels, with Jefferson displaying an astonishing versatility both in the roles he filled and as an inventor of stage effects, Cooper essaying Hamlet for the first time at the Chestnut, and Wood acting Townly in *The Provoked Husband* and the exacting part of Othello.

Criticisms of these performances are comparatively rare. *The Theatrical Censor and Critical Miscellany* had ceased publication with its December 30, 1806 number; and the *Port Folio* was devoting itself to learned essays on literature, drama and music, with a leaven of such contemporary wit as told of a widow objecting to the burial of her husband next to a man who had died of the smallpox as her husband had never had it, or as flashed in quaint epitaphs such as the verses to the memory of:

Kate Smith, a wealthy Spinster, aged four-score,
Who'd many aches, and fancy'd many more;

Knitting her friends to the grave, with a church-yard cough,
Long hung she on death's nose, 'till one March morn
There came a wind north-east, and blew her off,
Leaving her Potticary quite forlorn.

It may have been an imaginary epitaph but the essays must have led to a deeper appreciation of the dramas, songs, and dances being offered. The musical program was as ambitious as ever, with Mrs. Wilmot on June 24, as Peggy in *The Country Girl,* singing "Get Away Sorrow," the words by a gentleman of Philadelphia, the music by Bray. On July 8 Mrs. Warren as Juliana, in Act IV of *The Honeymoon,* sang the much liked "At the Front of the Cottage," and again on December 28 and February 24. After *Venice Preserved* on September 22 at the Southwark, Wilmot sang a new comic song, "Dan the Waiter's Journey to London," and Mrs. Wilmot, as Lucy in *The Virgin Unmasked,* sang "additional songs," repeated as such on September 30. On September 26 Durang sang a comic song in *Olla Podrida,* and Barrett, as the 1st Irishman in *Rosina,* the additional song of "Go to the Devil and Shake Yourself." On October 12, the last night at the Southwark, Barrett sang "The Hobbies" after *Lover's Vows,* Wilmot "The Man of All Trades" and Mrs. Wilmot "Get Away Sorrow," composed by Bray and written by a gentleman of Philadelphia.

Back at the Chestnut Mrs. Seymour, as Taffline in *Town and Country,* sang a song by Reinagle on December 26, January 11, and February 10 and 19. On January 1 "Girl of My Heart" was sung by Webster, and the catch of "Old Thomas Day" was sung in *Harlequin Dr. Faustus.* The usual dirge accompanied the funeral procession in Act V of *Romeo and Juliet* on January 8. Mrs. Warren, on January 15, sang "Gentle Cousin Julia" as Louisa Davenant in *The Soldier's Daughter;* and Cross as Mephistopheles and Mrs. Mills as Helen of Troy in *Harlequin Dr. Faustus* contributed

Audience Reaction: The Embargo

"songs" and a "song" respectively. Gillingham created musical atmosphere with a violin concerto in the "grand gala" in the Doge's palace in Act V of *Abaellino* on January 22.

After *Reconciliation,* on February 8, there was a comic song by Bray; and on March 2 "The Twins of Latona," by Robbins as Fitzroy in *The Poor Soldier.* On March 4 Mrs. Melmoth was billed as Olivia Wyndham in *Time's a Telltale,* "with the original song and music." On March 7 Mrs. Warren sang a song as Laetitia Hardy in Act IV of *The Belle's Stratagem* and, in the course of *Harlequin in the Moon,* Jefferson repeated "Giles Scroggins' Ghost." After *Mahomet,* on March 11, Bray sang "Madame Fig's Gala"; and, in an *Olla Podrida* or "Dish of All Sorts," on March 12, Mrs. Melmoth sang "Drimindoo" and Webster " Cushlamacree." On March 16, Jefferson, as Strop in *The Embargo,* sang "Twiggle and a Friz," and Webster, as Louis de Linval in *Youth, Love and Folly,* "Wander No More My Love." On March 18, in *The Anniversary of Shelah,* Robbins sang "The Standard of Freedom," Jefferson sang "Knowing Joe" and, at the end of *Town and Country* on March 23, "Captain Wattle and Miss Roe." After *The Provoked Husband,* on March 30, Mrs. Seymour sang "Sweet Lilies and Roses" and Webster "The Maid of Lodi," and on April 6, "by particular desire," the song of "Faithless Emma." After *Adrian and Orilla,* on April 1, Mrs. Mills sang the favorite "Turn Minutes to Seconds."

Among the dances old favorites were holding their own. The country dance by the characters accompanying the ploughing match in Act II of *Speed the Plough* was repeated on June 29 and December 7. The country dance was introduced at the end of Act IV of *The Honeymoon* on July 8, December 28, and February 24. After *The Peasant of the Alps,* on October 12, there was a gavotte. The juveniles of the company appeared in a number of characteristic dances: in a setting called the Temple of Liberty, concluding

Harlequin Hurley Burley on July 4, in Act II of *The Soldier's Return* on December 9, after *Adrian and Orilla* on February 22, and in Act I of a *Tale of Mystery* on March 9. Master F. Durang danced a hornpipe after *The Busybody* on July 10 and another after *Adrian and Orilla* on April 9.

In *Harlequin Dr. Faustus* on January 1 and 15 Masters Harris and Cunningham and Mr. Williams appeared in "The Dance of the Furies"; and on January 1 Masters F. Durang and T. Jefferson danced a comic dwarf dance. On March 4 the juveniles danced in a fête in Act II of *Time's a Telltale* and, on March 11, in a dance of cupids in Act I of *Cymon and Sylvia*. There was a characteristic dance composed by Francis in Act II of *The Fortress* on March 16 and another dance in which Master Durang and Miss Hunt performed a double hornpipe. The juveniles (Harris, Durang, Cunningham, the Misses Hunt and Mullin) danced an Irish lilt in *The Anniversary of Shelah* on March 18. In Act II of *The Soldier's Return,* on March 30, there was a characteristic dance; and, in the course of *The Sailor's Landlady,* on April 8, a triple hornpipe by Masters Harris and Durang and Miss Hunt, a fling by Masters Jefferson and A. Durang, and a reel by the characters.

In the season there were comparatively few scheduled recitations. After *The Children in the Wood* on July 8, Mrs. Wilmot gave "The Seven Ages of Women" and Collins' "Ode on the Passions." At the Southwark, after *Venice Preserved* on September 22, McKenzie recited "The Snowstorm"; and, as a part of *Olla Podrida,* on September 26, the thirteen-year-old Barrett "The Grecian Fabulist" and his father "Monsieur Tonson." After *Lovers' Vows,* on October 12, Mrs. Wilmot repeated the "Seven Ages," Mrs. Barrett recited Collins' "Ode," and her son, by particular desire, "Alonzo and Imogen."

At the Chestnut, on February 8, Bernard gave "The

Rambles of Dennis Brulgruddery"; on March 12, as a part of *Olla Podrida,* Mrs. Melmoth recited "The Portrait Painter," in which she portrayed the characters of a beau, a belle, a fine lady, a miser, a glutton, two speculators, an honest sailor, his sweetheart, and "her own"; and on March 30 Mrs. Melmoth recited "The Blackbirds."

In the season, which ended April 21, 1808, Warren and Wood had succeeded in maintaining a fair degree of order despite the turbulence of the times. It was their reward for an effort to anticipate unhappy contingencies and to make the theatre more comfortable and beautiful. On April 2 they assured the public that the visiting Oneidas, in presenting their War Dance, War Song, and Manner of Fighting, would wound no "feelings of delicacy" by their appearance and conduct; and it was announced that two figures, Comedy and Tragedy, recently completed by Rush, would be placed in the niches in front of the Chestnut. Fate decreed that they would symbolize the loss of two of the best known living figures on the American stage—one at the age of seventy-three and retired but the other only thirty-eight and in the full possession of her powers. Lewis Hallam died on November 1; and theatregoers who had seen her as Desdemona on April 20 were shocked to learn that Mrs. Warren had succumbed on June 28, presumably of a heart attack, while with the company in Alexandria.

10

Panoply
1808-1809

WAR OR EVEN a threat of war usually brings with it a love of pageantry. Before long the "War Hawks," Calhoun and Clay, were to harry the peaceful Madison into hostilities with England, considered a greater enemy than France for attaching the bodies of American seamen, an unpardonable offense to recently liberated America; and a growing love of spectacle was increased by a martial spirit in large measure responsible for the declaration of war against Britain on June 18, 1812.

There had been no regular circus company since the destruction of Rickett's and the bankruptcy of Lailson; and Don Leonis, Spanish consul, felt the time was ripe to invite a Spanish company to set up headquarters in Philadelphia. The building they opened in the spring of 1809, under the aegis of Pepin & Breschard as "The New Circus," was especially constructed for their purpose. The dome over its ring rose eighty feet above the northeast corner of Walnut and Ninth streets. Unlike the ventriloquism, magic shows, exhibitions of strange animals, tight-rope and sword-swallowing acts occasionally offered at the Southwark, the bills of Pepin & Breschard were serious competition for the Chestnut. Pepin, native Philadelphia and Acadian descendant, "whether on foot or on horseback," writes a contemporary, showed "the port of a king," receiving tumultuous applause as, garbed "in the costume of a Gallic field-marshal," he appeared at the circus, later enlarged and renamed the Walnut.

Warren and Wood, in planning the season which opened on November 7, 1808, were evidently anticipating a rivalry they had reason to fear. "The coffee room for the accommodation of the ladies," ran their advertisement for the opening night, "has been finished at great expense and will be ready for their reception." In addition to Mrs. Warren, the theatre had lost Cain and Woodham, who had both died in the summer; but Cain, though remarkably juvenile in appearance and possessing a fine voice and an ability thought equal to Wood's, had been a heavy drinker. As for Woodham, although a good musician, he was only an indifferent actor.

To replace Mrs. Warren the managers had secured Mrs. Barrett of the New York and Charleston theatres, who made her appearance on November 9, after an absence of six years, as Elvira in *Pizarro*; and they had also engaged Mrs. Stanley of Covent Garden to play Mrs. Warren's roles of Lady Teazle, Lady Townly in *The Provoked Husband,* Juliana in *The Honeymoon,* and Donna Violante in *The Wonder,* in a four-night engagement beginning December 5. Although this engagement was to prove a disappointment, Mrs. Green, the whilom Miss Williams of Wignell's first company, absent five years, lived up to her reputation for beauty and talent as the Widow Cheerly in *The Soldier's Daughter* and Margaretta in *No Song No Supper* on November 7; and there was a successful engagement with Harwood, beginning on January 25 and exhibiting him in the exacting roles of Dennis Brulgruddery in *John Bull,* Dr. Pangloss in *The Heir at Law,* Sir Callaghan in *Love à La Mode,* Sheva in *The Jew,* Sir David in *Ways and Means* and, on January 30 (three roles in one night), Rostrum in *Secrets Worth Knowing,* Sir Fretful in *The Critic*—albeit only in part—and Looney in *The Review.* In the course of two engagements, the ubiquitous Cooper, capable of playing two nights in Philadelphia and two nights the same week in New York, added to his usual Shakespearean repertory the role of Antony in *Julius Caesar,* acted in Philadelphia for the first time on December 16.

There were a dozen of Shakespeare's plays to discuss as the ladies sipped their coffee between the acts; and, in addition to *Julius Caesar,* fourteen pieces were presented for the first time in Philadelphia and two for the first in America. Outstanding among them were the plays that satisfied the current taste for spectacle. On January 2, 1809, Sheridan's "operatic romance" of *The Forty Thieves* revealed what had led to its performance at Drury Lane for "upwards of 200 nights to most crowded houses."

The scenery, machinery, dresses, and decorations were entirely new, the dances under the direction of Francis, and the "battle" and "marches" composed by the versatile Durang. Scene I was a coral-colored fairy grotto affording a view of a silver lake bounded by immense rocks. To the chorus of "Fairy of the Glassy Lake," Ardanelle the fairy, appears in her sea-shell chariot drawn by two white swans. Gossamer, another fairy, and a nymph, naiads, and sylphs attend her. Ardanelle vows to protect Ali Baba and his family from the enchanter Orchobrand and, with a wave of her wand, as "part of the scene opens," discloses Ali Baba and his son Ganem, with their old horse, repairing to their daily task of wood-cutting. There follows a scene in a wood, with Ali Baba, Jefferson playing the part, singing "To a Woodman's Hut There Came One Day," another in the garden and piazza of Cassim Baba's house in which Cogia, the wife of Ali Baba, sings "Ah Where Can I Turn for Relief," and another scene inside the cottage of Ali Baba, in which Morgiana and Cogia rendered the duet of "When O'er the Sunshine Clouds Are Cast."

Scene V was particularly elaborate, a robber's cave in a forest. The robbers arrive to the chant of "Pronounce the charm and split the rock." Their captain, Abdallah, cries the familiar "Open Sesame," the bandits conceal their booty inside the cave revealed by the parting of the rock and depart to the chorus of "Like the Wind Driven Snow," but not before a robber on guard has discovered the ax of Ali Baba beneath a tree in which he has taken refuge and they threaten to kill him.

In scenes that follow, Cogia sings "Last Night I Sate Me Down and Cried" and joins with Ali Baba in the duet of "While Poor the Spirit Flags." There was a chorus of furies and fiends in Orchobrand's abode, "Strike the World with Fear and Wonder," another duet by Morgiana and Ganem, "Ah Cruel Maid So Soon Retiring," a song by Morgiana, "Ah Little Blind Boy," and a song by Mustapha, a cobbler, "Last Week I Took a Wife." Cogia, Ganem, and Morgiana, as played by Mrs. Green, gave a tambourine dance.

The last scene was billed as the first of its kind ever attempted in America. Done completely in transparency, it represented the Lake Fairy's Palace of Jasper. Gold wreaths entwined columns joined by oblong transparent squares of various colors. The finale was a dance in which the former Miss Hunt, now the bride of Bray, the actor-composer, displayed her maturing powers. A record of twelve performances rewarded the managers for the pains they had taken with *The Forty Thieves.*

The tragedy of *Adelgitha,* current in London, was another of the new offerings elaborately presented, with scenes in the chapel and shrine of St. Hilda, in the Port of Orranto, in a cavern as seen through a natural arch, and in a Gothic hall, where a grand banquet ended, on January 20, with a martial ballad or chorus, "Conquer or Perish." On February 6 *Tekeli,* one of three new melodramas, struck a martial and inferentially patriotic note in a genre become popular. It had scenic effects such as windmill and watermill in operation and a dance by a corps de ballet. On March 17 *The Lady of the Rock* pictured the moods of sea and mountain in a Scotch melodrama featuring a rendition by the orchestra of the Scotch battle music called the "Piebrach," used in assembling the clans of the Campbells and McLeans. Artists and musicians again combined their efforts in the production of *The Wood Daemon* on April 10, three days before the season's end; but the melodrama was repeated only twice the following season despite its ambitious scenery, a characteristic dance, its chorus of "Strike, Minstrels Strike," in Act II, Scene II, and a pageant of the Four Seasons, proof that mere elaborateness seldom makes for success in the theatre.

In view of the trend of events the managers might have preferred a few of the new American plays to such dull importations as *The Wood Daemon.* On February 20 and March 29 they had scheduled American premières for *The School for Prodigals* and *The Wounded Huzzar,* both by J. Hutton of Philadelphia; but it had probably been out of the sense of duty prompting them on January 18 to appropriate the evening's profits for the relief of distressed sailors and their families in one of Philadelphia's severest winters. Yet they were fingering the public pulse. They had presented *Bunker Hill* on January 14, with Trumbull's painting of the death of General Warren again exhibited at its conclusion; and, on February 22, offered Dunlap's *Glory of Columbia,* with the interlude of singing, dancing, and recitation including *The Spirit of Independence,* in which there was an emblematic transparency of the "Genius of America." On March 4, when Madison became president, the managers presented *The Independence of Columbia,* a "grand olio" in honor of the day.

In offering such widely varied entertainment, Warren and Wood could draw upon talents of an unusually versatile company, among them Bray who, recently married to his charming little dancer, Miss Hunt, was capable of composing the overture and accompaniments for *Who Pays the Piper?,* which he translated for his benefit on March 25.

Reinagle was ailing; but, with such ability at the disposal of the managers, the season's music maintained a high level. Among the incidental songs was Jacobs', as Joe Mizzen in *Sailors on Shore,* on January 18; and on March 8, after *Which is the Man?,* "Miss Deborah Diddle," "Sir Gilbert-Go-Softly of Gooseberry Hall," "Master Jackey Gilpin's Intended Journey to Brighton," by Jefferson, and "Feyther and I," by Mr. [?] Bray.

On March 11, after *The Count of Narbonne,* there were "Giles Scroggins' Ghost" by Jefferson and "The Yorkshire Irishman" by Bray. On March 13, after *Hamlet,* Jefferson sang "The Cosmetic Doctor" and on March 15, after *The Benevolent Merchant,* the song of "Knowing Joe." Bray sang "Madame Fig's Gala." On March 17, *St. Patrick's Day,* Jacobs sang "The Standard of Freedom." There was a "solemn dirge" in Act II of *The Surrender of Calais* on March 18, and, after *First Love* on March 24, Jefferson sang a comic song, and, after *The Honeymoon* on April 1, "Let us All Be Unhappy Together."

Additional dances included a Country Dance by the characters at the end of Act IV of *The Honeymoon* on December 10 and April 1, a Country Dance accompanying the ploughing match in Act II of *Speed the Plough* on December 23, and, on the occasion of the sailor's benefit, January 18, a triple hornpipe by Masters Harris and C. and F. Durang.

There was a dance of Indians, evidently just actors, at the end of Act I of *The Indian Princess* on February 1 and, on March 17, an Irish Lilt to conclude *St. Patrick's Day.*

The recitations were an epilogue appropriate to *The School for Scandal,* on December 5, "The Seven Ages of Women" after *The Honeymoon* on December 10, and "The Standard of Freedom," in the character of the Genius of Liberty, after *The Wonder,* on December 12, (all by Mrs. Stanley); "The Secrets of Masonry Developed Through the Magic Influence of Jyce's Ring" by Barrett on March 11; "Ode to Freedom" spoken by Cone after Jefferson's song on March 13; "Belles Have at Ye All" by Mrs. Wilmot after *The Benevolent Merchant* on March 15; and, after *First Love* on March 24, an address written by a gentleman of Philadelphia and delivered by Green's lovely daughter, who was to lose her life a little over two years later in the fire that engulfed the Richmond Theatre.

Death seemed to hang in the air. Even before the Chestnut reopened on November 20, 1809, it was to claim three of the performers. Barrett, "Young Roscius'" father, passed away on November 18; and on the same day, September 21, there fell a double blow when Harwood, only thirty-nine, died in Germantown, and Reinagle in Baltimore. The latter had been intimately associated with the Chestnut from the beginning. A personal friend of the younger Bach, he was a famed teacher of pianoforte, harpsichord, and violin, and a concert artist and composer of note. His bushy, powdered hair, large high forehead, and full round face, "illuminated by silver mounted spectacle glasses" would be poignantly missed; and patrons whom he had greeted as they entered their boxes would recall, with nostalgic moisture in their eyes, his gentle smirk and deepening dimple as he watched his old friend Gillingham, the orchestra leader, turn irritably from Handel and Mozart to direct his musicians in "The President's March."

11

Warren & Wood
1809-1810

WIGNELL, MRS. WARREN, Harwood, and Reinagle had all taken their final bows, but a fortnight after the opening of its 1809-1810 season, a star who was acclaimed the "American Roscius" appeared at the Chestnut. Making his entrance as Young Norval, on December 6, he interpreted nine roles, mostly difficult, in a period of sixteen days. They ranged from Frederick (in *Lovers' Vows*) to Hamlet, Rolla (in *Pizarro*) to Romeo. The new star was short but unusually handsome. In 1817 Eicholtz was to paint his oval face, with its dark eyes and hair curling high above the forehead and about the ears, and its sensuous bow of a mouth. At fourteen he had started a magazine, *The Thespian Mirror*; and now at eighteen, in the fall of 1809, "appeared," in the words of Charles Durang, a contemporary, "the epitome of Prince Hamlet in soul and manner." Hardinge returned on November 22, after four years' absence, and West made an initial bow at the Chestnut on November 24; but neither could compete with the gifted youth, a future playwright of note, author of "Home, Sweet Home," and distinguished member of America's diplomatic corps. Neither Cooper, in a seven- and eight-night engagement, nor Dwyer of the O'Dwyers of Tipperary who, upon his first appearance on April 21 as Belcour in *The West Indian,* literally electrified the audience with his Hibernian good looks, could dispel or even dim the impression the prodigy had made.

His name was John Howard Payne.

Even with war in the offing, his native birth (in New York City) had little to do with his success, which rested upon the brilliance of his performance. The British musicians had to reconcile themselves to playing American songs and the British actors to occasional demonstrations of patriotic fervor. But the common literary, if not the political heritage, of England and her former colonies was intact. It seemed proper, moreover, for English actors to play the Shakespear- ean roles; and Cooke, whom Sully painted as Richard III, was so incomparable as the hunchback that audiences toler- ated the great English tragedian and Bunker Hill veteran (it was said) though he dubbed Madison "contemptible king of the Yankee Doodles" and refused to perform in his presence only a year before the outbreak of hostilities.

In the season of 1809-1810 nine of Shakespeare's plays were presented and there were other plays or entertainments belonging as much to a common heritage. *The Foundling of the Forest,* with its "Castle Garden" and melodramatic story, was of appeal to audiences on both sides of the Atlantic, and *Mother Goose* to the universal heart of childhood. Given its American première at the Chestnut on February 5, the latter (a pantomime) had a record of five performances. The artists accorded it their best, with a village in storm and sunrise, a view of "Mother Goose's Habitation," a mermaid's cave, and a "Submarine Palace, the wings or sides of which are Dolphins. In the perspective [is] a tripod of them and two recesses or alcoves, in each of which is seen a mermaid busily employed in combing her hair. The whole terminates, states the advertisement, "with a distant view of the sea, with the sun setting," adding "This is one of the most magnificent scenes ever exhibited in this theatre." For good measure or a sop to the parents of the youngsters present, the artists included a view of the Rising Sun Tavern on the Germantown road and of the Statehouse garden. On February 21, the pantomime was acted first so the children could be bundled off to bed at a decent hour; but the theatre's youngsters must have lost some needed sleep when, on March 28, they played all the roles in *Miss in Her Teens*.

Three nights later the managers again exhibited a local scene and struck a patriotic chord. After *The Foundling of the Forest* there was an "interlude interspersed with scenery, singing and dancing" and including a "grand panoramic view of the Schuylkill Bridge at the Falls." This beautiful scene, explained a bill, occupies the greater part of the stage, taking its range from near the front to the extremity. "In the course of the interlude the full length transparency of the immortal Washington which was exhibited at the Mansion House on February 22 [was] introduced with considerable alterations and improvements bearing the motto 'The name of American ought always to exalt the Just pride of patriotism.'" There was a comic song, "Little Jane of the Mill," sung by Mrs. Wilmot.

The interlude concluded with a grand characteristic dance by the corps de ballet, composed by Mr. Francis, in which they held aloft labels bearing the now famous "First in War, First in Peace and First in the Hearts of His Countrymen."

Near the season's end, on April 18, there was a return to the martial note in the romantic play of *The Africans*.

Despite the uncertainties of the times the season's bills included a dozen pieces new to Philadelphia and the usual number of songs, with Jefferson the most frequent interpreter. On March 14, after *Man and Wife,* he sang "How to Nail 'Em," and, in parody of Mrs. Wilmot's "Nobody Coming to Marry Me," the song of "Nobody Coming to Bury Me"; he repeated "How to Nail 'Em" after *The Count of Narbonne* on March 17 and *The Foundling of the Forest* on March 23. After the latter on March 19, Jefferson sang Dibdin's comic song of "The Waggoner" and, as Tristram Fickle in *The Weathercock,* the song of "Captain Wattle and Miss Roe." After *Grieving's a Folly,* on March 30, he sang "Knowing Joe"; and after *The Honeymoon,* on April 2, "Giles Scroggins' Ghost."

West, the newcomer, sang a comic song as Hawbuck in *Town and Country* on November 24, and after *The Foundling of the Forest* on April 16, another "descriptive of the London Ballad Singers." On March 16, after *The Iron Chest,* he sang an "antique song written in 1572" called "Hard Times or Always Agrumbling." On November 24, Mrs. Seymour sang a song as Taffline in *Town and Country.* Mrs. Wilmot sang songs as Little Pickle in *The Spoiled Child* on December 11 and March 5, "Sandy O'er the Lee" after *The Foundling of the Forest* on March 23, and "Sweet Bird," accompanied by Gillingham, after *The Honeymoon* on April 2.

The returning Hardinge sang "The Twins of Latona" as Fitzroy in *The Poor Soldier* on January 27 and, after *Grieving's a Folly* on March 30, C. Dibdin's "favorite Irish song" of "The World's a Good Thing." On December 1, Gillingham played a violin concerto as background music for a grand gala in the palace of the Doge of Venice in Act V of *Abaellino* and, in Act II of *The Lady of the Rock* the orchestra played "the celebrated Scotch Battle Music called the Piebrach for assembling the clans of the Campbells and McLeans."

In this season most of the incidental dancing was done

by a lightfoot lad named Whale, billed as the "Infant Vestris" and making his first appearance on November 29. After *Pizarro* on December 15 he danced a new Scotch *pas seul* by his father; and, after *The Iron Chest,* on March 16, a Scotch *pas seul.* After *Barbarossa,* on December 20, and in the masquerade of Act I of *Romeo and Juliet,* on December 22 and after *Douglas* on December 16, he danced a new *pas seul* by his father. After *Henry IV, Part I,* on January 10, and after *The Count of Narbonne* on March 17, he danced Madame Parisot's Hornpipe. On January 13, after *The Wheel of Fortune,* he danced a new garland dance. After *The Robbers,* on January 19, the boy danced a *pas seul*; after *The Foundling of the Forest* on March 12 an Irish jig, accompanied by W. Whale, his five-year-old brother; and another *pas seul* in a characteristic ballet by six warriors in Act II of *The Foundling of the Forest* on March 19. After *Grieving's a Folly* on March 30, he danced a new Scotch *pas seul.* On April 2 Mlle. Parisot's shawl dance as "performed by her at the Opera Houses in London and Paris with a most unbounded applause," and, after *The Foundling of the Forest* on April 16, a "new grand *pas seul,*" partly identified as a repetition of the shawl dance were given. On November 27 and January 17, Act I of *Ella Rosenberg* ended with a dance.

The recitations were Collins' Ode by Mrs. Barrett, after *The Count of Narbonne* on March 17; and, on March 19, "Ode to American Freedom" by Cone and, on March 23, "Alonzo and Imogen," by McKenzie, both after a performance of *The Foundling of the Forest.*

With the end of the season of 1809-1810, what might be termed the most crucial period in the history of the American theatre drew to a close. The war against them had ended in victory for the playhouses in Boston, New York, and Philadelphia. Occasional riots occurred and the trollopes still were flamboyantly present in the pit; but the "leather breeches beaux" of a previous era, as William Dunlap pictures them, "with their powdered wigs, long stiff skirted coats and waistcoats, with flaps reaching nearly to the knees of their inexpressibles, their silk stockings, short-quartered shoes, silver or paste buckles," had vanished as completely as had the Hessian with his towering, brass-fronted cap, mustachios colored with the same material that he used on his shoes, his hair plastered with tallow and flour and tightly drawn into a long appendage reaching from the back of his head to his waist. Neither Dunlap, the New York manager, nor Wignell and Reinagle would have wanted to tolerate the bucks who had once crowded and ogled the actresses on the stage and bought box tickets for the purpose of gaining admission behind the scenes.

General Washington, whose legend was growing rapidly, had helped to make the theatre respectable, and even the status of the actor had definitely changed for the better. It was no longer necessary for a player to explain his ownership of a coach, as the gouty Henry once did, with an heraldic symbol of crossed crutches and the motto on its door reading "This or These." The actor himself was partially to be credited with his improved position in society. Sir John Oldmixon, Bath beau, with the snuff-box which he opened, tapped, and presented with the air of a finished gentleman, was an endearingly nostalgic figure, but it was now absurd for an actor to draw attention to himself, as Hodgkinson used to do, by appearing on the street with powdered curls and long braided hair twisted into a knot or club behind. The happy result was that the player had come to be accepted as a regular member of society.

The theatre itself had become a recognized institution. With their disciplined theatrical corps and a playhouse to which it was safer for a man to take his wife and children, Warren and Wood had won the city's patronage and a national reputation for the Chestnut by bringing to Philadelphia the best of the Drury Lane and Covent Garden plays—

tragedies by Lewis, Home, Rowe, Lillo, and Otway; comedies by Farquhar, Reynolds, Mrs. Cowley, the Colmans, and Sheridan; farces by Mrs. Inchbald and O'Keeffe; Gay's *Beggar's Opera* and comic operas by the Dibdins and Hoare. In the decade establishing the firm that was to last until 1826, the managers staged 109 performances of Shakespeare, introducing to Philadelphia *King John, Henry VIII, Henry V,* and *Julius Caesar* and producing *Henry IV, Part II* for the first time in America.

The faith of Lewis Hallam, Jr., "Father of the American stage," and the lure of the New World had brought to its shores the players who could interpret the great roles—Fennell to play Richard, Macbeth, Lear; Cooper to play Richard, Macbeth, Hamlet; Mrs. Warren to play Lady Macbeth, Ophelia, Juliet.

The cultural influence of the Chestnut had been far-reaching. In an era of sailing ships and stage-coaches Milbourne's and Holland's scenes of lonely German forests and snow-covered steppes excited the imagination and must have been an inspiration to artists and lovers of art. Plays acted at the Chestnut were avidly read when published. Books of songs from its operas were purchased for Philadelphia drawing-rooms; and Reinagle, the Chestnut's co-manager, Gillingham, its orchestra leader, and Victor Pelissier, a member of its orchestra, instructed on the pianoforte, violin and French horn. Raynor Taylor, organist and erstwhile teacher of Reinagle, and the famed Benjamin Carr, composer, opera and concert singer, pianist, music publisher and dealer, both associated with the theatre, were active in fostering a love and understanding of music. Francis, composer and director of many of the Chestnut's ballets and pantomimes, conducted a school of dancing in which he taught the city's belles a grace for which they came to be noted. Fennell and Cooper gave recitations that were lessons in fine diction.

Few monuments have been erected to the men and women

who acted out a segment of their lives within the walls of the Chestnut, and the whereabouts of their final resting-places are mostly unknown. The managers, the stars, the prompters who stood with book in hand and rang the bells for "up and down curtain," "up and down lamps," "signaled the fiddlers for accompanying music or the carpenters to simulate thunder and lightning with their cannon balls and sheets of tin, the message carriers, the dram drinkers, the candle snuffers, all are but shadows to be rescued only from rapidly fading pages; but in their day they played an important role in helping to interpret the culture of the Old World and in fostering the culture of the New. And, though most of them seemed hopelessly British to the Sons of Liberty, one and all they created their own particular roles in the drama of our early history by their service in helping to awaken and unify American national spirit.

Epilogue

Almost complete files of Claypoole's *American Daily Advertiser,* Poulson's *American Daily Advertiser,* the *Aurora* and the *United States Gazette,* their rag paper in excellent condition, are available in the Historical Society of Pennsylvania and the Ridgeway libraries. The theatre advertisements they contain, including the songs, dances, and recitations as well as the pieces performed, are an accurate guide as to what occurred in the playhouses, save for the rare last-minute changes in the bills, sometimes recorded in the *Port Folio,* a contemporary periodical. The newspapers of the period are a novelist's paradise. In their pages we can side with the partisans of Adams or Jefferson, ride in the stages with the Philadelphian of their day, drink his claret and malaga, visit the Leopard tavern or the Shakespeare Hotel with him, or the museum in the State House (now Independence Hall), scan his favorite books—the English, Latin and Greek classics, books of science, or *Memoirs of the Courts of Dresden, Warsaw and Vienna,* in 2 vols.—attend his Assemblies, go with his children to the Dame Schools or Dancing Academies, or, in lighter mood, gape at the wax figures, "African lions," whales, or "Grisley Bears from Missouri" exhibited at the time, or chuckle at the contemporary humor of such an epitaph as

> Here lies the body of Jacob Sneer,
>   Who had a mouth from ear to ear;
> Reader, tread lightly on his sod,
>   For if he gapes—you're gone by G—— [*sic*].

For what this Philadelphian thought of the entertainment afforded in the Southwark or the Chestnut Street Theatre we can turn to the *Port Folio, The Theatrical Censor,* and *The Theatrical Censor and Critical Miscellany.*

As for the books that acquaint us with Philadelphia's early Nineteenth Century Theatre, we have William B. Wood's *Personal Recollections of the Stage,* published in 1855, a mellow though occasionally inaccurate volume written in the manager's declining years; William Dunlap's *A History of the American Theatre,* published in 1832; and Thomas Clark Pollock's *The American Theatre in the Eighteenth Century,* published by the University of Pennsylvania Press in 1933, an entertainingly written book in which there is mention of many of the plays and players later produced or presented. Available, too, though still unpublished, is William Warren's record of his managerial experience, now reposing in the Library of Congress, a manuscript quoted in Volume Two of Odell's *Annals of the New York Stage* and in the present author's *Old Drury of Philadelphia* (University of Pennsylvania Press, 1932), a book embodying Wood's "account book" of his stewardship at the Chestnut.

Concentrating more on the drama itself are Arthur Hobson Quinn's indispensable *A History of the American Drama from the Beginning to the Civil War,* published by Harper & Brothers in 1923, and George C. D. Odell's compendious *Annals of the New York Stage,* Volume Two (1789 to

1821), published by the Columbia University Press in 1927, in which many of the actors known to Philadelphians of the period move through familiar roles. For a record of the English drama currently produced in America we have Allardyce Nicoll's invaluable *A History of Late Eighteenth Century Drama,* (Cambridge University, 1937) and *A History of Early Nineteenth Century Drama* (Macmillan, 1930) covering respectively the periods of 1790 to 1800 and 1800 to 1850.

Colorful contemporary accounts of the players who made this drama live are *Retrospections of America, 1797-1800,* by the talented John Bernard (Farmer Ashfield, Sir Peter Teazle, Young Wilding) published by Harper & Brothers in 1887, and the little-known *An Apology for the Life of James Fennell,* as written by himself, a friend of Joseph Hopkinson. Elizabethan in tone and companion to *A Groat's Worth of Wit,* Robert Greene's unhappy confession, this volume (Philadelphia, 1814) lifts the curtain on Philadelphia of the plague and the career of a physical and mental giant who could play the great roles of the Bard, recite for university audiences, invent a water alarm-clock for his immediate need, but who surrendered to the bottle in an uneven battle with his unruly spirit.

There are two books especially important for the information they contain about the music of the period, O. G. Sonneck's *Early Opera in America,* published by Schirmer in 1915, and John Tasker Howard's *Our American Music,* published by Crowell in 1930.

Books about Philadelphia are legion and many of them have to do at least partly with the city in the first decade of the nineteenth century. *Moreau de St. Méry's American Journey,* as translated and edited by Kenneth Roberts and Anna M. Roberts (Doubleday & Co., Inc., 1947) runs close enough to the period (1798) to reveal what Philadelphia was like at the time Washington graced the Southwark with his presence. Elizabeth Drinker's *Journal* is similarly helpful. J. Thomas Scharf and Thompson Westcott's *A History of Philadelphia,* 1609-1884 (3 vols., Everts & Co., Philadelphia, 1884) is a reliable baedeker of old Philadelphia, covering every aspect of its life, industrial, political, and social. Less known but quaintly interesting are two other books, John F. Watson's *Annals of Philadelphia and Pennsylvania in the Olden Time* (Philadelphia, 1877-1879) and *The Picture of Philadelphia,* 1811 to 1831, by James Mease and Thomas Porter, in which we rattle over its cobbled streets in one of the "396" four-wheeled carriages or "588" two-wheeled chaises that vied with the public hacks in the Philadelphia of 1801 or shiver before the hickory, oak, or maple wood fires of its citizens as in 1810 they awaited the removal of "obstructions" in the Lehigh and the inland navigation that would bring them adequate supplies of the much-needed coal. In the "picture," published in Philadelphia in 1831, we go the rounds with the "32" watchmen who cry the hour for their $14 a month, with 27 cents extra for every city lamp they light and the "gratuity of a great coat." All of these Philadelphia books are to be found in the Historical Society of Pennsylvania, Ridgeway, or University of Pennsylvania library. A glimpse of Philadelphia with its Northern Liberties and Southwark districts is obtainable in a map of the city, 1796, preserved in the manuscript department of the Historical Society of Pennsylvania.

Most to be cherished of all the sources, however, are Charles Durang's articles on the Philadelphia stage (1749-1855), as printed in the *Sunday Dispatch* beginning May 7, 1854. While occasionally inaccurate and incomplete in their coverage, these recollections of a member of a family once prominent in the theatre are unique among the records of what took place on the Philadelphia stage and of the people who trod and patronized it a century and more ago. Like Warren's journal the material for a valuable and fascinating

Epilogue

book, they remain unpublished, pasted up and bound in volumes little consulted, in the Historical Society of Pennsylvania and University of Pennsylvania libraries, in the latter of which they are extra-illustrated with rare and interesting old prints of playhouses and players.

R.D.J.

Appendix A. Plays, Ballets, Pantomimes, and Musical Entertainments 1800-1810

(**B** stands for ballet, **C** for comedy, **CO** for comic opera, **F** for farce, **HD** for historical drama, **M** for melodrama, **MD** for musical drama, **MF** for musical farce, **O** for opera, **P** for pantomime and **T** for tragedy. Further identification is from the advertisements. The name of the author and the number of performances are given.)

Abaellino, **T**, Dunlap, 10
Adelgitha, **T**, Lewis, 5
Adelmorn, romantic drama, Lewis, 5
The Adopted Child, **MD**, Birch, 5
Adrian and Orilla, **play**, Dimond, 11
The Africans, **play**, Colman the Younger, 2
The Agreeable Surprise, **CO**, O'Keeffe, 12
Aladdin or The Wonderful Lamp, **P**, O'Keeffe, 3
Alexander the Great, **T**, Lee, 14
Alfonso, King of Castile, **T**, Lewis, 8
All the World's a Stage, **F**, Jackman, 1
American Heroes, **dance**, Francis, 1
American Heroine or Harlequin Neptune, **P**, 1
The American Sailor, **interlude**, 1
American Tars in Tripoli, **F**, 2

The Deuce Is In Him, **C,** Colman the Elder, 1
The Devil Among Tailors, **humorous piece,** 2
The Devil to Pay, **MF,** Coffey, 6
The Devil to Pay or The Cobbler at Home, **C,** 1
The Distressed Mother, **T,** Phillips, 4
The Doctor and the Apothecary, **CO,** Cobb, 3
Don Juan, **tragic pantomime,** Delphini, 5
Donald Mackintosh's Travels, **interlude taken from The Register Office,** Reed, 1
The Double Disguise, **O,** Mrs. Hook, 2
Douglas, **T,** Home, 8
The Dramatist, **C,** Reynolds, 8
Dr. Last's Examination, **C,** from Foote's *The Devil upon Two Sticks,* 3
The Duenna, **CO,** Sheridan, 3
Duplicity, **C,** Holcroft, 2
The Earl of Essex, **T,** Jones, 5
The East Indian, **C,** Lewis, 2
Easter Gambols, **pantomimical dance,** Francis, 1
Easter Holidays, **F,** 1
Edwy and Elgiva, **T,** Ingersoll, 2
The Election, **musical prelude,** by Reinagle, 1

Ella Rosenberg, **M,** Kenney, 4
The Embargo, **interlude,** Barker, 1
The Enraged Musician, **MF,** 1
The Enterprise, **entertainment, dialogue, singing, spectacle,** 1
Everyone Has His Fault, **C,** Inchbald, 7
The Fair Penitent, **T,** Rowe, 3
The Fairy Favor or Edgar and Emmeline, **dramatic romance,** Hawksworth, 1
False and True, **C,** Moulton, 2
False Shame, **C,** Kotzebue, 1
Falstaff's Wedding, **C,** Kendrick, 1
The Farmer, **CO,** O'Keeffe, 7
The Fashionable Lover, **C,** 1
Feast of Anacreon, **interlude,** 1
The Feast of Reason and the Flow of Soul, **dramatic olio,** 1
The Federal Oath, **pantomimical sketch,** 1
Fête des Vendages, **ballet P,** 1
The Fingerpost, **C,** T. Dibdin, 3
First Love, **C,** Cumberland, 1
Five Thousand a Year, **C,** C. Dibdin, 1
The Flitch of Bacon, **MF,** Bate, 3

Appendix A

The Follies of a Day, C, Holcroft from Beaumarchais, 5
Folly As It Flies, C, Reynolds, 4
The Fortress, M, Hook, 8
Fortune's Frolic, F, Allingham, 16
The Forty Thieves, operatic romance, Sheridan, 14
The Foundling of the Forest, play, Dimond, 10
Fourth of July, fête, 1
The Fox Chase, C, Breck, 2
The Gamester, T, Moore, 7
The Generous Farmer, musical piece, Mrs. Melmoth, 1
The Gentle Shepherd, Scots pastoral, Tickell from Ramsay, 2
George Barnwell, T, Lillo, 10
The Ghost, F, Mrs. Centlivre, 6
The Glory of Columbia, historical play, Dunlap, 4
The Grateful Lion or Harlequin Shipwrecked, P, 3
The Grecian Daughter, T, Murphy, 5
Gretna Green, MF, O'Keeffe, 1
Grieving's a Folly, C, Leigh, 1
The Guardian, C, Garrick, 1
Guilty or Not Guilty, C, T. Dibdin, 3
Gustavus Vasa, T. Brooke, 5
Half an Hour After Supper, interlude, 1

Hamlet, T, Shakespeare, 18
Harlequin Doctor, P, 1
Harlequin Dr. Faustus, P, Francis, 4
Harlequin Freemason, P, 2
Harlequin Hurley Burley, pantomimical sketch, Francis, 1
Harlequin Hurry Scurry, P, Francis, 5
Harlequin Mariner or The Miller Deceived, P, 1
Harlequin in the Moon, pantomimical dance, Francis, 7
Harlequin Neptune or The Temple of Hymen, P, 2
Harlequin Prisoner, pygmy P, 3
Harlequin Recruit, P, Robertson, 1
Harlequin Restored, P, 1
Harlequin Tammany, P, 1
Harlequin Turned Washerwoman, pantomimical interlude, 1
Harlequin's Almanac, P, T. Dibdin, 3
Harlequin's Invasion, "speaking" P, Garrick, 2
Harlequin's Vagaries, pantomimical dance, Francis, 1
The Haunted Tower, CO, Cobb, 2
Hear Both Sides, C, Holcroft, 1
Hearts of Oak, C, Allingham, 2

The Heir at Law, C, Colman the Younger, 8
Henry IV, I, historical play, Shakespeare, 7
Henry IV, II, historical play, Shakespeare, 2
Henry V, historical play, Shakespeare, 1
Henry VIII, historical play, Shakespeare, 4
Henry the Second, T, Hull, 1
Hercules and Omphale, P, 9
The Hero of the North, historical play, Dimond, 3
He's Much to Blame, C, Holcroft, 1
He Would Be a Soldier, C, Pilon, 6
The Highland Reel, CO, O'Keeffe, 10
High Life Below Stairs, F, Townley, 10
A Hint to Husbands, C, Cumberland, 1
The Honest Thieves, F, Knight, 4
The Honest Yorkshireman, new musical entertainment, Carey, 1
The Honey Moon, C, Tobin, 14
The Horse and the Widow, F, T. Dibdin from Kotzebue, 5
A House to be Sold, MF, Cobb, 6
The Humorist, F, Cobb, 3

The Hunter of the Alps, drama, Dimond, 9
Hurley Burley, pantomimical sketch, Francis, 1
Il Bondocani, dramatic romance, T. Dibdin, 3
I'll Tell You What, C, Mrs. Inchbald, 1
Independence of Columbia, grand olio, 2
The Indian Chief or The Choice of Harlequin, P, 1
The Indian Princess, M, Barker, 2
Inkle and Yarico, CO, G. Colman the Younger, 6
The Invisible Girl, musical entertainment, Hook, 2
Irish Fair, comic dance, Francis, 1
The Irish Widow, F, Garrick, 1
The Irishman in London, F, Macready, 8
The Iron Chest, play, Colman the Younger, 1
Isabella, T, Southerne, 4
Is He a Prince? F, Hoare, 1
Jack in Distress or The Sailor's Rendezvous, pantomime ballad, 1
Jacob Gawkey's Rambles, 1
Jane Shore, T, Rowe, 5
The Jealous Wife, C, Colman the Elder, 2
The Jew, C, Cumberland, 4
The Jew and the Doctor, F, T. Dibdin, 9

Appendix A

Joanne of Montfaucon, **dramatic romance,** Cumberland from Kotzebue, 2
John Bull, **C,** Colman the Younger, 12
Julius Caesar, **T,** Shakespeare, 2
July 4, 1776, **characteristic piece told in action,** 1
Killing No Murder, **MF,** Hook, 5
The King and the Miller of Mansfield, **dramatic satire,** Dodsley, 6
King John, **T,** Shakespeare, 2
King Lear, **T,** Shakespeare, 4
Knights of Calatrava, **heroic pantomimical dance,** T. Dibdin, 1
Know Your Own Mind, **C,** Murphy, 1
La Chantreuse [*sic*] **dance,** Lalliot, 1
La Foret Noire or The Natural Son, **P,** 2
La Perouse, **pantomimical drama,** Fawcett, 9
Lady of the Rock, **M,** Holcroft, 7
Laugh When You Can, **C,** Reynolds, 1
The Law of Lombardy, **C,** Jephson, 3
Lewis of Monte Blanco, **M,** Dunlap, 1
The Liar, **C,** Foote, 3
Liberal Opinions, **C,** T. Dibdin, 2 (Under the Title of

The School for Prejudice, November 4, 9, 1801)
Liberty in Louisiana, **C,** Workman, 1
The Lie of the Day, **C,** O'Keeffe, 1
Life, **C,** Reynolds, 3
Linco's Travels, **speaking piece,** Garrick, 1
Lionel and Clarissa, **O,** Bickerstaffe, 1
Lock and Key, **CO,** Hoare, 8
Lodoiska, **romantic drama,** John Philip Kemble, 1
The London Hermit, **C,** O'Keeffe, 7
The Lord of the Manor, **C,** O'Keeffe, 1
Love à La Mode, **F,** Macklin, 6
Love and Money, **interlude,** Benson, 1
Love for Love I Promise Him, **musical entertainment,** Kenney, 1
Love in a Camp, **CO,** O'Keeffe, 2
Love in a Village, **O,** Bickerstaffe, 2
Love Laughs at Locksmiths, **MF,** Colman the Younger, 9
Love Makes a Man, **C,** Cibber, 3
Lovers' Quarrels, **F,** King, 8 (Under title of *Like Master Like Man, August* 13, 1808)
Lovers' Vows, **C,** Kotzebue, 8
The Lying Valet, **F,** Garrick, 2

Macbeth, **T,** Shakespeare, 12
Mahomet, **T,** Miller, 5
The Maid of Bristol, **play,** Boaden, 2
The Maid of the Oaks, **C,** Burgoyne, 1
Man and Wife, **C,** Arnold, 1
The Man of Ten Thousand, **C,** Holcroft, 1
The Man of the World, **C,** Macklin, 2
Management, **C,** Reynolds, 4
The Manager in Distress, **prelude,** Colman the Elder, 5
Marian, **CO,** Mrs. Brooke, 2
The Marriage Promise, **C,** Allingham, 3
Mary Queen of Scots, **T,** St. John (?), 1
The Masked Friend, **C,** Holcroft, 1
Matrimony, **MF,** Kenney, 2
The May-Day Dower, **CO,** 3
The Mayor of Garrat, **F,** Foote, 8
Melocosmiotes, **songs and recitations,** 3
The Merchant of Venice, **C,** Shakespeare, 7
The Merry Girl, **ballet dance,** 1
The Merry Wives of Windsor, **C,** Shakespeare, 9
Midas, **burletta,** O'Hara, 1
The Midnight Hour, **C,** Mrs. Inchbald from Beaumarchais, 5

The Miraculous Mill, **comic pantomimical ballet,** Francis, 3
Mirth by Midnight, **Scots dance,** Francis, 2
The Miser, **C,** Fielding from Molière, 1
Miss in Her Teens, **F,** Garrick, 4
The Mock Doctor, **F,** Fielding, 4
Modern Antiques, **F,** O'Keeffe, 8
A Mogul Tale, **F,** Mrs. Inchbald, 2
Monoco Indians or A Trip to Niagara, (?), 1
A Monody Sacred to the Memory of Washington, 1
More Ways than One, **C,** Mrs. Cowley, 1
Mother Goose, **pantomimical operatical romance,** T. Dibdin, 5
The Mountaineers, **C,** Colman the Younger, 13
The Mourning Bride, **T,** Congreve, 4
Mrs. Wiggins, **comic piece,** Allingham (?), 1
Much Ado about Nothing, **C,** Shakespeare, 3
My Grandmother, **MF,** Hoare, 5
The Mysteries of the Castle, **play,** Andrews, 1
The Natural Son, **C,** Cumberland, 2

Appendix A

The Naval Pillar, **musical entertainment,** T. Dibdin, 4
Netley Abbey, **operatic F,** Pearce, 1
A New Wreath for American Tars, **dramatic sketch,** 2
Next Door Neighbors, **C,** Mrs. Inchbald, 1
No Song No Supper, **CO,** Hoare, 10
Notoriety, **C,** Reynolds, 1
Obi, **pantomimical drama,** Fawcett, 7
Of Age Tomorrow, **CO,** T. Dibdin, 5 (English version of *The Wild Goose Chase*)
The Old Maid, **F,** Murphy, 3
Olla Podrida, 3
The Orphan, **T,** Otway, 2
Othello, **T,** Shakespeare, 8
The Padlock, **CO,** Bickerstaffe, 5
The Paragraph, **musical entertainment,** Hoare, 2
Patrick in Prussia, **CO,** O'Keeffe, 1
Paul and Virginia, **O,** Cobb, 10
The Peasant of the Alps, **P,** 1
A Peep Behind the Curtain, **F,** Garrick, 2
Peeping Tom, **C,** O'Keeffe, 1
Percy, **T,** Miss More, 2
Peru Avenged, **T,** Murphy, 1
Phantasmagori, **grand spectacle,** 1
Pizarro, **T,** Sheridan from Kotzebue, 22

The Point of Honor, **drama from the French,** C. Kemble, 13
The Poor Gentleman, **C,** Colman the Younger, 12
The Poor Soldier, **CO,** O'Keeffe, 12 (January 13, 1803, under title of *Patrick's Return*)
The Portrait of Cervantes, **F,** C. Kemble, 4
The Positive Man, **MF,** O'Keeffe, 1
The Prisoner at Large, **F,** O'Keeffe, 9
The Prize, **CO,** Hoare, 13
The Procession, **grand spectacle,** Francis, 1
The Provoked Husband, **C,** Cibber, 4
The Purse, **MD,** Cross, 9
A Quarter of an Hour Before Dinner, **interlude,** Rose, 1
The Rage, **C,** Reynolds, 1
Raising the Wind, **F,** Kenney, 12
Ramal Droog, **F,** Cobb, 1
Rambles of Dennis Brulgruddery, **comic interlude,** 1
Raymond and Agnes, **P,** taken partly from Lewis' novel *The Monk,* 3
Reconciliation, **C,** T. Dibdin from Kotzebue, 12
The Recruiting Officer, **C** Farquhar, 2
The Recruiting Serjeant, **CO,** (?), Dibdin, 1

Red Cross Knights, **play,** G. Holman from Schiller's *The Robbers,* 3
The Register Office, **comic sketch,** Reed, 2
Reparation, **C,** 1
Retaliation, **F,** MacNally, 1
The Revenge, **T,** Young, 6
The Review, **F,** Colman the Younger (?), 12
Richard Coeur de Lion, **historical MD,** Burgoyne from Sedaine, 1
Richard III, **T,** Shakespeare, 11
The Rival Sisters, **ballet dance,** Francis, 1
The Rival Soldiers, **MF,** O'Keeffe, 13
The Rivals, **C,** Sheridan, 4
The Road to Ruin, **C,** Holcroft, 9
The Robbers, **T,** from Schiller, 5
Robin Hood, **CO,** MacNally, 5
Robinson Crusoe or Harlequin Friday, **P,** 3
The Roman Father, **T,** Whitehead, 3
Romeo and Juliet, **T,** Shakespeare, 11
The Romp, **CO,** Bickerstaffe, 10
Rosina, **CO,** Mrs. Brooke, 11
Rosina or The Harvest Moon, **ballad,** 2
Rugantino, **M,** Lewis, 1
Rule a Wife and Have a Wife, **C,** Beaumont and Fletcher, 5
Rural Merriment, **dance,** 1
The Sailor's Daughter, **C,** Cumberland, 6
The Sailor's Garland, **interlude,** 1
The Sailor's Landlady, **B,** Francis, 2
Sailors on Shore, **interlude,** 3
The Sailor's Return from Tripoli, **pantomimical dance,** Francis, 4
St. Crispin's Day or Hunt the Slipper, **B,** 1
St. David's Day, **musical entertainment,** T. Dibdin, 6
St. Patrick's Day, **F,** Sheridan, 6
Sancho Turned Governor, 1
The Scheming Milliners, **pantomimical dance,** Francis, 3
The School for Arrogance, **C,** Holcroft, 1
The School for Friends, **C,** Miss Chambers, 1
The School for Prejudice, **C,** T. Dibdin, 2 (Changed from *Liberal Opinions*)
The School for Prodigals, **C,** Hutton, 1
The School for Reform, **C,** Morton, 5
The School for Scandal, **C,** Sheridan, 10
The School for Soldiers or West Point Preserved, **P,** 2

Appendix A

The Seaside Story, **new piece,** Dimond, 1
The Secret, **C,** Morris, 9
Secrets Worth Knowing, **C,** Morton, 4
Selima and Azor, **Persian tale from the French** by Sheridan, 1
The Shakespearean Jubilee, **entertainment of music, dialogue and spectacle,** 5
She Stoops to Conquer, **C,** Goldsmith, 8
She Would and She Would Not, **C,** Cibber, 1
Shelty's Frolic, **B,** Francis, 5
Shelty's Travels and A Voyage to America, **recitation,** Dunlap (?), 2
The Shipwreck, **CO,** Colman the Younger, 10
The Sicilian Romance, **MD,** Henry, 1
The Siege of Belgrade, **CO,** Cobb, 4
Siege of Oxydrace, **grand heroic spectacle taken from** *Alexander the Great,* 1
Sighs, **C,** Kotzebue, 2
The Sixty-Third Letter, **MF,** Oulton, 5
The Soldier's Daughter, **C,** Cherry, 7
The Soldier's Return, **CO,** Hook, 4
The Son-in-law, **CO,** O'Keeffe, 2

Sons of Apollo, **interlude,** 2
The Spanish Barber, **CO,** Colman the Elder, 6
Spanish Dollars, **MF,** Cherry, 1
Speed the Plough, **C,** Morton, 23
The Spirit of Independence, **interlude,** 2
The Spoiled Child, **F,** Bickerstaffe, 16
The Stranger, **C,** Dunlap from Kotzebue, 11
The Sultan, **F,** Bickerstaffe, 4
Surrender of Calais, **historical play,** Colman the Younger, 2
The Suspicious Husband, **C,** Hoadly, 4
Sylvester Daggerwood, **comic interlude,** 14
A Tale of Mystery, **M,** Holcroft, 14
A Tale of Terror, **M,** based partly on Molière's play *The Feast of the Statue,* Henry Siddons, 9
Tancred and Sigismunda, **T,** Thompson, 4
Tears and Smiles, **C,** Barker, 3
Tekeli, **M,** Hook, 6
The Tempest, **C,** Shakespeare (with additions from Dryden as compiled by J. C. Kemble), 1
The Temple of Flora, **masque,** 1

Theseus and Ariadna, **M,** 1
Thirty Thousand, **O,** T. Dibdin, 1
Three and the Deuce, **MF,** Hoare, 1
Three Weeks after Marriage, **C,** Murphy, 11
Time's a Tell-Tale, **C,** Henry Siddons, 1
'Tis All a Farce, **F,** Allingham, 5
To Marry or Not to Marry, **C,** Mrs. Inchbald, 1
The Tobacco Box, **musical dialogue,** 1
Tom Thumb the Great, **burletta,** Fielding, 10
Tony Lumpkin in Town, **F,** O'Keeffe, 1
Too Many Cooks, **musical entertainment,** Kenney, 6
The Touchstone of Truth or Harlequin shipwrecked, **speaking P,** 2
Town and Country, **C,** Morton, 10
The Travellers, **O,** Cherry, 6
A Trip to Fontainbleau, **MF,** O'Keeffe, 3
A Trip to Scarborough or The Man of Quality, Sheridan from Van Brugh, 3
The Tripolitan Prize, **CO,** altered from *The Veteran Tar* of S. J. Arnold, 1
The Turnpike Gate, **CO,** Knight, 12

Two Huntsman or The Death of the Bear, **ballad,** 1
The Two Misers, **ballad,** 1
The Two Misers or The Merry Girl, **pantomimical ballet dance,** 1
Two Per Cent, **interlude,** 1
Two Strings to Your Bow, **F,** Jephson, 2
The United Volunteers, **country dance,** 1
Valentine and Orson, **M,** T. Dibdin, 8
The Valiant Soldiers or The Two Robbers, **P,** 2
Venice Preserved, **T,** Otway, 10
The Village Lawyer, **F,** Macready, 14 (Billed August 30, 1800, as *Mad or Not Mad*)
Vintner in the Suds, **interlude,** Ward (?), 2 (Probably second episode of farce, *The Vintner Trick'd or The White Cloud Chas'd*)
The Virgin in the Sun, **play,** Dunlap from Kotzebue, 10
The Virgin Unmasked, **F,** Fielding, 2
The Voice of Nature, **M,** Dunlap, 6
The Votary of Wealth, **C,** Holman, 3
The Walking Statue, **interlude,** Hill, 1
The Wanderer, **play, C,** Kemble from Kotzebue, 1

Appendix A 139

The Wandering Jew, **F,** Franklin, 2
The Waterman, **M,** C. Dibdin, 5
The Watermelon Fair or Summer's Vagaries, comic rural dance, 1
The Way to Get Married, **C,** Morton, 7
The Way to Keep Him, **C,** Murphy, 1
Ways and Means, **C,** Colman the Younger, 5
We Fly by Night, **MF,** Colman the Younger, 4
The Weathercock, **F,** Allingham, 12
The Wedding Ring, **C,** Mrs. Inchbald, 6
A Wedding in Wales, **C,** Stock, 2
The West Indian, **C,** Cumberland, 8
What Would the Man Be At?, **F,** 3
The Wheel of Fortune, **C,** Cumberland, 8
The Wheel of Truth, **F,** Fennell, 1
Which Is the Man?, **C,** Mrs. Cowley, 3
Whitsuntide Holiday, **B,** 1
Who Pays the Piper, **CO,** translated from the French by Mrs. Bray, 1
Who Wants a Guinea?, **C,** Colman the Younger, 1
Who Wins?, musical entertainment, 2
Who's the Dupe?, **F,** Mrs. Cowley, 7
Wicklow Mountains, musical entertainment, O'Keeffe, 2
The Widow of Malabar, **T,** Humphrey, 2
The Wife of Two Husbands, **MD,** from Pixérécourt by Cobb, 2
The Wild Goose Chase, **C,** Dunlap from Kotzebue, 3
The Will, **C,** Reynolds, 3
Will for the Deed, **C,** T. Dibdin, 1
William Penn or The Landing of Our Forefathers, speaking piece, 2
Windsor Wags, **F,** 2
Wives As They Were and Maids As They Are, **C,** Mrs. Inchbald, 6
The Wonder, **C,** Mrs. Centlivre, 5
The Wood Daemon, **M,** Lewis, 5
Word to the Wise, **C,** Kelly, 1
The World, **C,** Kenney, 1
The Wounded Hussar, play, Hutton, 1
The Young Hussar, **O,** Dimond, 2
Youth, Love and Folly, **MF,** Dimond, 4
Zorinski, **MD,** Morton, 2

Appendix B. Performers

(Names by previous marriages appear in parenthesis.)

Miss Arnold	Master	Gibbons
Bailey	Cunningham	Gibson
Barnet	Dalmon	Gillingham
Barrett	Darley	Mrs. Gillingham
Mrs. Barrett	Mrs. Darley (Miss	Goodwin
Master Barrett	E. Westray)	Mrs. Graham
Miss Baxter	Darling	Miss Graham
Bernard	Mrs. Doctor	Master Gray
Blissett	Downie	Green
Bray	Mrs. Downie	Mrs. Green
Brien	Drummond	Hallam
Briers	J. Dudley	Hammond
Miss Broadhurst	Durang	Hardinge
Mrs. Brumley	Master A. Durang	Harris
Burd	Master C. Durang	Master Harris
Cain	Master F. Durang	Harwood
Charnock	Master T. Durang	Hodgkinson
Mrs. Coffee	Dwyer	Miss F.
Cone	Fennell	Hodgkinson
Cooper	Fox	Hogg
Cross	Francis	Hook
Cunningham	Mrs. Francis	Hopkins
Mrs. Cunningham	Fullerton	Miss Hoyden

Appendix B

Miss Hunt
Jacobs
Mrs. Jacobs
Jefferson
Mrs. Jefferson
Miss Jefferson
Master J. Jefferson
Johnson
Jones
Mrs. Jones
Miss Jones
Kenny
  (McKenney?)
L'Estrange
Master L'Estrange
Lewis
Mrs. Lynch
Master Lynch
Mrs. McDonald
McKenzie
McKnight
Miss McMullen
Maginnis
Mrs. Maginnis
Marshall
Mrs. Marshall
Mrs. Melmoth
Mestayer
Milbourne
Miller
Mills
Mrs. Mills
Mitchell
Morris
Mrs. Morris

Mrs. Oldmixon
Ormsby
Parsons
Master Payne
Miss Pettit
Miss R. Pettit
Poe
Mrs. Poe
Prigmore
Radcliff
Roach
Robbins
Robert
Rowson
Mrs. Rowson
Rutherford
Rutley
Mrs. Salmon
Miss Salmon
Sanderson
Saunders
Master
  Scribner (?)
Scriven
Miss Scriven
Miss
  Scrivener (?)
Serson
Seymour
Seymour 2nd.
Mrs. Seymour
Mrs. Shaw
Master Shaw
Soff
Miss K. Solomons

Mrs. Stanley
Mrs. Steward (?)
Mrs. Story
Mrs. Stuart
Taylor
Thornton
Twaits
Usher
Mrs. Usher
  (Mrs. Snowden)
Warrell
Mrs. Warrell
Warrell, Jr.
T. Warrell (?)
Warren
Mrs. Warren
  (Mrs. Merry,
  Mrs. Wignell)
Webster
West
Miss Westerly
Western
Wheatley
Whitlock
Mrs. Whitlock
Wignell
Williams
Wilmot
Mrs. Wilmot
Wolf
Wood
Mrs. Wood (Miss
  J. Westray)
Woodham
Mrs. Woodham

Index

Foreword

Changes in the names of players are often misleading and so, in appendix A, Miss Arnold also appears as Mrs. Poe, Miss Hunt as Mrs. Bray, and Mrs. Marshall as Mrs. Wilmot. As recorded, Mrs. Snowden became Mrs. Usher and Mrs. Merry, Mrs. Wignell and then Mrs. Warren. In the Index, the roles in the productions are omitted; but many of them are listed on the pages to which references are made after the names of the actors and actresses and many more, minor as well as major, appear in the advertisements mentioned in the Epilogue. With few exceptions, no more than a single reference is made to a play, dance, or song, when repeated, on a given page. It has occasionally been difficult to distinguish a few of the instrumental offerings from the recitations and the recitations from the songs, some of which remain unidentified. There must have been an accompaniment, perhaps by the orchestra, to the dirge at the end of *Romeo and Juliet;* and the Giles Scroggins and Dennis Brulgruddery recitations could have been fetching as vocal pieces. Idiosyncrasies in spelling, punctuation, and capitalization are from the text of the advertisements. All direct quotations from them have been reproduced to the letter. Current usage was rather fluid and capital letters may suggest the importance attached to that part of a bill. Place names of no significance have been omitted and in the Index there is obviously no account of any changes in the programs made too late to be reported in the press and due, perchance, to the exigencies of travel, sudden illness, or over-indulgence in the Leopard Tavern.

Index

Aaron, Miss, 64
Abaellino, 52, 53, 71, 103, 116
Adams, John (President), 19, 23, 29, 34
Adelgitha, 110
Adelmorn, 45
Adrian and Orilla, 98, 99, 100, 103, 104
Africans, The, 115
Alexander the Great, 31
Alfonzo, 53
American Daily Advertiser, 96
American Tars in Tripoli, 67, 68
André 38
Anniversary of Shelah, The, 99, 103, 104
Apology, 51
Argus (brig), 81
Arnold, Elizabeth (later Mrs Poe), 15, 21, 34, 37, 38
Artaxerxes, 33
Arthur and Emmeline, 67, 70, 73
As You Like It, 18

Bach, 112
Barbarossa, 87, 117
Barbary Pirates, 49, 67, 86
Barker, 97, 98
Barnett, 89
Barrett, 28, 37, 101, 102, 104, 112
Barrett, Mrs., 52, 101, 104, 107
Barrett, Master, 101, 104
Battle of Hexham, The, 36, 37, 42, 93
Battle of Prague, The, 83
Belle's Stratagem, The, 54, 103
Benevolent Merchant, The, 111
Bernard, 20, 23, 32, 33, 34, 41, 42, 43, 46, 48, 51, 54, 55, 59, 101, 104
Blind Bargain, The, 83

Blissett, 42, 48, 54, 59, 64, 68, 69, 70, 72, 77, 78, 79
Bluebeard, 19, 21, 30, 32, 41, 83
Blue Devils, 64
Bold Stroke for a Husband, A, 50
Bologno, Signor (Belogno), 89, 100
Bonaparte Mistaken, 56
Boston Theatre, 20, 101
Botheration, 28
Bray, 78, 80, 86, 87, 89, 91, 92, 93, 99, 102, 103, 111
Bray, Mrs. (formerly Miss Hunt), 109, 111
Brazen Mask, The, 81
Broadhurst, Miss, 22
Brown, Charles Brockden, 20
Bunker Hill or The Death of General Warren, 38, 49, 67, 110
Burke, Master, 38
Burr, Aaron, 66
Busby, Dr., 61
Busybody, The, 55, 93, 104
Byrne, 81

Cabinet, The, 92, 95
Cain, 33, 38, 40, 41, 42, 48, 50, 65, 70, 77, 79, 91, 95, 107
Caldwell, 89
Calhoun, 106
Captain Smith and the Princess Pocahontas, 74, 85
Carey, 20
Carmelite, The, 78
Carr, 48, 71
Carr, Benjamin, 119
Castle Spectre, The, 21, 34, 46, 52
Catch Club, The, 34, 72
Cato, 30
Center Square, 68
Chateaudun, 45

145

Chesapeake (frigate), 97
Chestnut Street Theatre, 17, 20, 25, 26, 34, 36, 37, 38, 49, 51, 52, 53, 57, 58, 59, 61, 62, 66, 67, 70, 71, 74, 76, 86, 95, 97, 100, 101, 102, 104, 107, 112, 113, 114, 118, 119, 120
Children in the wood, The, 104
Cincinnati (society), 66
Cinderella, 77, 80, 81, 90
Clandestine Marriage, The, 73, 93, 95, 101
Clark, 73
Clay, 106
Cleone, 70
Coelina, 61
Cole, John, 98
Colman (the Elder), 119
Colman (the Younger), 18, 39, 61, 119
Cone, 87, 91, 95, 99, 112
Cone (Junior), 99
Congress, 90
Constellation, The, or a Wreath for American Tars, 17
Constitution (frigate), 89
Cooke, 114
Cooper, 21, 23, 29, 32, 34, 36, 39, 40, 43, 46, 50, 52, 55, 58, 70, 73, 80, 90, 101, 108, 114, 119
Coriolanus, 18
Corsair, The, or The Tripolitan Robbers (from *Obi*), 48
Corsicans, The, 33
Count Benyowski, 56, 62
Counterfeit, The, 73
Count of Narbonne, The, 111, 116, 117
Country Girl, The, 41, 101, 102
Covent Garden, 18, 30, 61, 100, 118
Cowley, Mrs., 18, 119
Critic, The, 20, 30, 83, 108
Cross, 80, 99, 102
Cumberland, 18
Cunningham, 88
Cunningham, Mrs., 78, 80
Cunningham, Master, 94, 98, 104
Cure for the Heartache, A, 36, 46
Cymbeline, 43
Cymon and Sylvia, 104

Dances:
"Allemand en trois," 73
Ballet, 73; dance by a corps de ballet, 110; characteristic ballet, 115, 117
"Caledonian Frolic," 34
Characteristic dance, 54, 73, 65, 82, 84, 87, 89, 94, 103, 104, 110
"Corn Piece," 46
"Cotillion, Martial," 98
Country dance, 34; entitled "rural," 46; 54, 60, 61, 65, 72; new, 84; 94; "The United Volunteers," 98, 103, 111
Dance (unidentified), 27, 47, 62, 72, 104, 109, 117; of the cupids, 104; of the fairies, 73; Indian, 73; of Indians (actors?), 112; tambourine, 109; "Dance of the Furies, The," 104; Scots dance, 94
"Dwarf Dance, The, or The Whimsical Transformation," 95; comic dwarf dance, 104
"Fandango, Spanish," 34, 37; grand, 65; 73
Fling, 84, 88, 94, 104; "Highland Fling, The," 38, 94
"Four and Twenty Fiddlers," 27
"Garland" dance, 69, 73, 89; new, 117
Gavotte, new, 34, 38, 64, 103
Hornpipe, 27, 64, 72, 73, 89, 94; solo, 94, 98, 99, 104; double, 29, 46, 104; "The Jockey's Hornpipe," 65; "medley," 34; Sailors, 27; Scotch, 84; treble, 22; triple, 22, 34, 73, 84, 88, 104, 110
Irish Hay-Makers, 69; Irish Jig, 94, 117; Irish Lilt, 94, 104, 112
Madame Parisot's Hornpipe, 117
Mlle. Parisot's shawl dance, 117
La Chantreuse [sic], 84
Minuet, 34, 36; mock, 54;

＃ Index

Dances (Continued)
  mock, 73; mock, 84, 89;
  minuet de la cour, 34, 38, 54,
    64, 73, 89
  Pantomime, 60
  Pas de trois, 54, 65; pas "en
    militaire," 98; pas russe, 89;
    pas seul, 117; new grand,
    117; Scotch pas seul, 117;
    Scottish allegorical pas seul,
    89
  Pastoral, 60, 91
  Procession and dance, 73
  Reel, 73, 83, 84, 88, 104; high-
    land, 94; Scotch, 65; reels
    and strathspeys, 65
  Sailors on Shore, 68
  Sailor's Return from Tripoli,
    The (founded on The Sail-
    or's Landlady), 83
  Saraband, Spanish, 60
  "Savage Dance, The," 27
  "Statue" scene and dance, 94
  Strathspey, 34, 94
  War dance, 46, 105
Darley, 22, 33
Darley's son, 33
Davy, 69
Deaf and Dumb, 40
Deaf Lover, The, 50
Death of General Wolfe, The, 56
De Breuys, 82
Decatur, Captain, 67, 82, 87, 89, 94
Delaware Chiefs, 46
Dennie, Joseph ("Oliver Old-
  school"), 31, 32, 33, 39, 42, 43,
  44, 45, 46, 50, 76, 77
Dibdin, Charles 28, 116, 119
Dibdin, T., 21, 82, (T.?), 116
  (T.?), 119
Distressed Mother, The, 93, 94
Dorsey, 89
Dr. Last's Examination, 59
Donald Mackintosh's Travels (in-
  terlude from The Register Of-
  fice), 93
Don Leonis, 106
Double Disguise, The, 22
Douglas, 42, 77, 79, 101, 117
Downie, Mrs., 64
Dramatist, The, 53

Drinker, Elizabeth, 34, 49; Journal,
  25, 66
Drury Lane 18, 30, 61, 81, 108, 118
Dunlap, 16, 30, 58, 70, 110, 117,
  118
Durang, John, 26, 27, 28, 29, 34, 54,
  60, 73, 83, 88, 89, 98, 99, 100, 102,
  108
Durang, Mrs., 29, 64, 98
Durang, Master, 64, 65, 83, 84, 88,
  94, 98, 104
Durang, Master A., 84, 88, 89, 92,
  94, 99, 104
Durang, Charles, brief biography
  of, 88; as historian, 31, 97, 113;
  as Master C., 73, 89, 94, 98, 111
Durang, Master F., 73, 88, 89, 93,
  94, 98, 99, 104, 111
Dwyer, 114

Earl of Essex, The, 41, 42, 44
East Indian, The, 34
Eaton, 81, 82, 87, 94
Edwy and Elgiva, 30, 34
Eicholtz, 113
Election, The (verse), 38
Ella Rosenberg, 117
Embargo, The, 99, 103
Embargo Act, 86, 97
Enraged Musician, The, 44
Enterprise, The, or A Wreath for
  American Tars, 49

Fair Penitent, The, 20
False and True, 73
Farmer, The, 83
Farquhar, 119
Fawcett, 81
Feast of Anacreon, The, 64
Federal City, 23
Federal Oath, The, or The Inde-
  pendence of 1776, 49
Fennell, 51, 52, 53, 65, 79, 80, 85,
  90, 95, 119
First Love, 111
Folly as It Flies, 43
Fortress, The, 100, 104
Forty Thieves, The, 108, 109
Foundling of the Forest, The, 114,
  115, 116, 117
Fox, 22, 53, 54, 55, 60, 64

Fox Chase, The, 85
Francis, 22, 34, 38, 48, 53, 54, 62, 63, 64, 68, 69, 70, 72, 73, 82, 83, 84, 87, 88, 91, 94, 98, 99, 104, 108, 115, 119
Francis, Mrs., 23, 41, 42, 91
Fullerton, 36, 37, 40, 42

Generous Farmers, The, 91, 93, 94
Gentle Shepherd, The, 94
George Barnwell, 101
Gibbons, 40
Gillingham, 64, 71, 82, 91, 92, 93, 99, 103, 112, 116, 119
Glory of Columbia, The, 110
Green, 46, 54
Green, Mrs. (formerly Miss Williams), 107, 109
Green, Miss, 112
Grétry, 22
Grieving's a Folly, 116, 117
Gross, 91
Gustavus Vasa, 23

Hallam, 48, 54, 95, 105, 119
Hamilton, Alexander, 66
Hamlet, 46, 111 (*See* Cooper, 21, 46, 101, 119)
Hardinge, 59, 64, 67, 71, 72, 113, 116
Harford, C., 82, 93
Harlequin Dr. Faustus, 102, 104
Harlequin Freemason, 22
Harlequin Hurley Burley, 104
Harlequin Hurry Scurry, 33
Harlequin in the Moon, 103
Harlequin Mariner, 28
Harlequin Prisoner, 53
Harlequin Recruit, 37
Harlequin Restored, 64
Harlequin's Almanac, 53, 54, 55
Harris, Master, 34, 38, 47, 54, 64, 65, 72, 73, 83, 84, 88, 94, 98, 104, 111
Harwood, 79, 80, 83, 84, 88, 108, 112, 113
Harwood, C., 89
Haymarket, Little, 61
Heir at Law, The, 57, 79, 108
Henry, 118

Henry IV, Part I, 23, 43, 70, 90, 117
Henry IV, Part II, 52, 90, 119
Henry V, 119
Henry VIII, 53, 54, 119
Henry, Patrick, 48
Hercules and Omphale, 45
He Would Be a Soldier, 86
High Life Below Stairs, 36, 37, 54, 73, 84
Hoare, 119
Hodgkinson, 28, 29, 49, 52, 53, 54, 55, 84, 118
Hodgkinson Miss F., 84
Hogg, 53
Holcroft, Thomas, 61
Holland, 17, 21, 23, 30, 49, 53, 55, 61, 62, 68, 81, 87, 89, 119
Holliday Street Theatre (Baltimore), 88
Home, 119
"Home, Sweet Home," 38, 114
Honeymoon, The, 83, 84, 92, 94, 102, 103, 107, 111, 112, 116
Hopkins, 20, 22
Hopkinson, Joseph, 22
Hornet (sloop), 81
House to Be Sold, A, 70
Hunt, Miss (later Mrs. Bray), 47, 54, 64, 65, 72, 73, 79, 82, 83, 84, 88, 89, 94, 98, 99, 104
Hutchins, 26
Hutton, J., 110

Ignace's Dancing Academy, 51
Il Bondocani, 42, 45
Inchbald, Mrs., 18, 119
Independence of Columbia, The, 111
Indian Princess, The, 97, 112
Instrumental Performances:
    Accompaniment, 93, to "Sweet Bird," 116; on harp, 45; on pianoforte, 99, to *The Catch Club,* 72; to glee of "Red Cross Knights," 92; on trumpet, 82, 83, 93; to "The Glory of Columbia, Her Yeomanry," 89; to "The Standard of Freedom," 98
    Arrangement of music in *Mary, Queen of Scots,* 79

Index

Instrumental Performances (con'd)
  Concert of vocal and instrumental "musick," 82
  "Concertante with "pianoforte" and harp, 82; concerto on the violin, 82, 93, 103, 116
  Instrumental music, 71
  March (dead), for *Coriolanus*, 93; "President's March, The," 26, 48, 112; "Jefferson's March," by Reinagle, 47, 86; "Washington's March," 48, 67
  Orchestral parts by Reinagle of *La Perouse*, 69
  Overture (unidentified), 83; to *The Battle of Prague* (with trumpet and bugle horn obligato), 82; to Grétry's *Richard Coeur de Lion*, 22; "Masonic," by Reinagle, 64; "miscellaneous," 71; national, 68; "new medley," 83; to *Who Pays the Piper?* (with accompaniments), 111
  "Piebrach," 110, 116
  Prelude ("Masonic"), 45
  Trumpet and bugle horn obligato (in addition to above), 82
  "Yankee Doodle," 26, 67
Irish Haymakers, The, 94
Irish Widow, The, 64
Iron Chest, The, 116, 117
Irving, Washington, 32
Isabella 83, 93
Israel (person), 89
"Italian Fantoccina," 51

Jacob Gawkey's Travels (Rambles?), 22
Jacobs, 111
Jane Shore, 41
Jefferson, Joseph, 58, 64, 65, 71, 72, 73, 77, 82, 83, 84, 86, 87, 90, 91, 92, 93, 99, 101, 103, 109, 111, 116
Jefferson, Mrs., 59, 64
Jefferson, Master, 65, 84, 88, 104
Jefferson, Thomas (President), 29, 39, 51, 55, 58, 67, 97
Jew, The, 42, 59, 108

Joanna of Montfaucon, 44
John Bull, 56, 61, 64, 70, 83, 108
John Street, 58, 70
Jones, 40, 41, 42, 46, 48
Jones, Mrs., 41, 45, 46, 48, 49, 53, 54
Julius Caesar, 108, 119

Kean, Edmund, 32
Kemble, John, 20
King John, 20, 119 (*See* Cooper, 21)
King Lear (*See* Foreword to Index and Fennell, 119)
Knights of Calatrava, The, 62, 64, 65
Kotzebue, 21

Lady of the Rock, The, 110, 116
Lailson's, 25, 26, 106
Lalliet, M., 84
La Perouse, 69, 70, 76, 81, 90
La Vengeance (ship) 17
Law of Lombardy, The, 30
Lee, Henry, 16
Leopard (frigate) 97
Leopard Tavern, 28
Lewis, 62, 73, 119
Lewis of Monteblanco, 84
Liberal Opinions, 30
Liberty in Louisiana, 56, 66
Life, 46
Lillo, 119
L'Insurgente (frigate) 17
Lock and Key, 50
London Hermit, The, 38, 43
Louisiana (territory), 48
Louisiana Purchase, 66
Love à la Mode, 60, 108
Love and Money, 94
Love in a Village, 94
Love Makes a Man, 89
Lovers' Quarrels, 60
Lovers' Vows, 91, 102, 104, 113
Lynch, Master, 37, 45, 46

Macbeth, 43 (*See* Foreword to Index, Cooper, 21, 32, 52, 70, 80, 119, and Fennell, 119)
Macready, 57
McDonald, 37

McDonald, Mrs., 27
McGinnis, 59, 60
McGinnis, Mrs., 60
McKenzie, 70, 79, 85, 104
Madison, James (President), 106, 111, 114
Mahomet, 103
Maid of Bristol, The, 61
Man and Wife, 116
Manfredi, 61, 80
Marian, 94
Marriage Promise, The, 61
Marshall, Mrs. (later Mrs. Wilmot), 22
Mary, Queen of Scots, 77, 79
May-Day Dower, The, 83
Mayor of Garrat, The, 93
Melmoth, Mrs., 78, 79, 80, 84, 86, 90, 91, 93, 98, 103, 105
Melocosmiotes, 55, 93, 94
Merchant of Venice, The, 43
Merry, Mrs. (later Mrs. Wignell, Mrs. Warren), 18, 29, 32, 41, 42, 44, 50, 51
Merry Wives of Windsor, The, 43, 70
Michault, 71
Milbourne, 17, 21, 23, 30, 48, 49, 55, 61, 68, 119
Mills, 87, 91, 94, 95, 98, 99
Mills, Mrs., 87, 98, 102, 103
Mineckey, 98
Miraculous Mill, The, 73
Miss in Her Teens, 87, 115
Mitchell, 22
Moore, 82
Moorhead, 69
Moreton, 50
Morris, Mrs., 59, 64
Moses, Miss, 64
Mother Goose, 114
Mountaineers, The, 29, 36, 37, 59, 60, 65, 73
Mourning Bride, The, 41
Much Ado about Nothing, 64
Mullen, Miss, 89, 98, 104

Napoleon, 55, 60
"National Theatre," 30
Nautilus (schooner), 81
Naval Pillar, The, 17

Nelson, Lord, 67
"New Circus, The," 106
New Wreath for American Tars, A, 67
North Point, Md., 88
No Song No Supper, 107

O'Bannon, 81, 82
Obi, or Three-Fingered Jack, 39, 45
Oeller's Hotel, 20
O'Keeffe, 18, 119
Oldmixon, Mrs., 22, 33, 37, 40, 41, 42, 44, 45, 53, 54, 55, 64, 70, 71
Oldmixon, Sir John, 118
Olla Podrida, 93, 94, 103, 104, 105
Oneidas, 105
Othello (performer), 59
Othello (See Foreword to Index, Cooper, 32, 70, and Fennell, 80)
Otway, 119

Park, 18, 36, 58, 70, 90
Paul and Virginia, 62, 65, 80, 83, 84
Payne, Master, 38, 114
Peale, Charles Willson, 20, 37
Peasant of the Alps, The, 103
Peeping Tom of Coventry, 91
Pelissier, Victor, 119
Penn Treaty Oak, 68
Pennsylvania Freemason's Hall, 54
Pepin (& Breschard), 106, 107
Phantasmagori, 100
Philadelphia, 29, 34, 68
Philadelphia (ship), 67
Pike, Zebulon, 74
Pizarro, 21, 31, 33, 44, 83, 92, 107, 113, 117
Placide, 37
Poe, 87
Poe, Edgar Allan, 15, 20
Poe, Mrs. (formerly Miss Arnold), 86, 87
Point of Honor, The, 70
Poor Gentleman, The, 39, 73, 78, 95
Poor Soldier, The, 17, 33, 51, 60, 103, 116
Popoote, Miss, 27
Port Folio, 32, 39, 76, 79, 80, 87, 101
Positive Man, The, 22

Index

Potomac, 68
Preble, Commodore, 67, 82, 87, 89, 90, 94
Prigmore, 29
Provoked Husband, The, 101, 103, 107
Purse, The, or The Benevolent Tar, 41, 78, 83
"Pyramids of Egypt, The," 27

Rachel, Miss, 64
Raising the Wind, 78
Randolph, John, 19
Rannie, 51, 61
Raymond and Agnes, or The Bleeding Nun (from Lewis' *The Monk*), 62, 69
Recitations:
  Address, 84, 112; Masonic, 55; occasional, 55, 91, 95; to the town, 55
  "Alonzo and Imogene," 23, 34, 54, 73, 117
  "Belles Have at Ye All," 112
  "Birth, Christening, Marriage and Other Family Misfortunes of Dennis Brulgruddery, The," 84 (*See* "Songs")
  "Blackbirds, The," 86, 105
  "Comic Tale of Monsieur Tonson, The," 54, 104
  "Dennis Brulgruddery's Description of Pizarro," 84
  "Dialogue between a Fop and a Master Mason, A," 65
  "Dissertation on Hobby Horses, The," 34, 46, 55
  "Dutchman and His Wife, The," 60
  Epilogue, Dr. Goldsmith's, 28, 95; to *The Carmelite,* 84; to *The East Indian,* 34; to *Edwy and Elgiva,* 34; to *The School for Scandal,* 112; to *Such Things Are,* 55; to *A Wedding in Wales,* 46
  "Eulogium on the American Worthies," 86, 98
  Eulogy on Masonry, 65
  "Freedom on Thy Fertile Plains," 95
  "Friends, Romans, Countrymen," 95
  "Giles Jallup (Gallop) and Brown Sally Green," 34, 55; "comic Parody on," 72, 73
  "Grecian Fabulist, The," 104
  "Lectures on Heads," 28
  Ode, Collins', 117; Dryden's, 84; "of Alexander's Feast," Dryden's, 95; on the Passions, Collins', 104; "to Freedom," 112; to "American Freedom," 117; to American liberty, 49, 55; to St. Cecilia's Day, Dryden's, 46
  Oration in honor of Louisiana and the United States, 67
  "Portrait Painter, The," 105
  Prologue, occasional, 60; to *The Fox Chase,* 85; to *Life,* 46; to *Management,* 34; "new," to *The Way to Keep Him,* 38; to *Tears and Smiles,* 91
  "Rambles of Dennis Brulgruddery, The," 105
  "Secrets of Masonry Developed through the Magic Influence of Jyce's Ring, The," 112
  "Seven Ages," 27
  "Seven Ages of Women, The," 104, 112
  "Snow-storm, The," 104
  "Standard of Freedom, The," 112
  "Water Bottle, The, or The Miraculous Cure," 23
Reconciliation, 21, 103
Recruiting Officer, The, 28
Red Cross Knights, 49
Register Office, The, 93
Reinagle, 15, 16, 17, 18, 22, 24, 30, 36, 44, 50, 52, 54, 55, 59, 61, 64, 67, 69, 71, 72, 79, 86, 88, 90, 94, 111, 112, 113, 118, 119
Reinagle, Hugh, 61, 68, 81
Reparation, 44
Revenge, The, 53, 60, 79
Review, The, 108

Reynolds, 119
Richard III, 65 (See Foreword to Index, Cooper, 32, 119, and Fennell, 119)
Richmond Theatre, 20
Rickett's Circus, 20, 25, 26, 106
Rivals, The, 101
Rival Sisters, The, 94
Rival Soldiers, The, 33, 50
Road to Ruin, The, 33, 77
Robbers, The, 117
Robbins, (Robins), 17, 23, 54, 61, 68, 69, 71, 72, 81, 82, 83, 87, 89, 91, 92, 95, 98, 99, 100, 103
Robertson 36, 37
Robinson, 64
Roman Father, The, 16
Roly Poly, 37
Robin Hood, 72
Romeo and Juliet, 62, 64, 72, 73, 82, 83, 94, 95, 98, 117
Rosina, 50, 101
Rowe, 119
Rowson, 27, 28
Rowson, Mrs., 27, 28, 29
Rule a Wife and Have a Wife, 18
Rush, William, 20, 105
Rutherford, 77, 99

Sailor's Daughter, A, 70, 83
Sailor's Landlady, The, 104
Sailors on Shore, 69, 111,
Sailor's Return from Tripoli, The, 88
St. David's Day, 30, 42, 45
St. Patrick's Day, 111, 112
Sancho Turned Governor, 53
San Domingo, 18, 55
Scheming Milliners, The, 65
School for Prejudice, The, 40
School for Prodigals, The, 110
School for Scandal, The, 17, 58, 77, 112
Scriven, Miss, 47, 72, 89, 94
Secret, The, 41
Secrets Worth Knowing, 65, 108
Selima and Azur, 73
Serson, 101
Seymour, 71
Seymour, Mrs., 72, 82, 86, 98, 99, 102, 103, 116

Shakespeare (on performances of), 119
Shakespeare Jubilee, The, 70
Shaw, Mrs., 32, 36, 54, 73
Shawnee Chiefs, 46
Sheridan, 21, 108, 119
She Would and She Would Not, 59
Shipwreck, The, 45, 50, 79
Siddons, Mrs., 43
Siege of Belgrade, The, 30, 33
Siege of Oxydrace, 31, 32
Sixty-Third Letter, The, 52
Smith (J. B.), 81, 90
Snowden, Mrs., 64
Soldier's Daughter, The, 107
Soldier's Return, The, 104
Solomon(s), Miss, 22, 34, 48, 64, 65
Songs:
"Adventures of a Yorkshire Potato Merchant," 87; "Ah Cruel Maid So Soon Retiring," 109; "Ah Hapless Is the Maiden," 45; "Ah Little Blind Boy," 109; "Ah Where Can I Turn for Relief," 109; "All's Well" (duet), 92; "At the Front of the Cottage," 92, 102; "The Auctioneer," 54
"Bay of Biscay, The," 87; "Bird Song, The," 92; "Birth, Christening, Marriage and Other Family Misfortunes of Dennis Brulgruddery, The," 71; "Black-Eyed Susan," 93; "Blue Bells of Scotland, The," 45, 60; "Bonny Bet," 83; "Bonny Bold Soldier, A," 87, 98; "Bright Beaming Star," 69
"Caleb Quotem's Avocations," 64, 68; "Captain Wattle and Miss Roe (Rose), 72, 103, 116; "Cashlamacree," 103; "Catch Club, The," 22, 72; chorus (grand), 60; "Clown's Description of London, A," 60; "Come, Jolly Boys, Let's Sailors Be,"

Index

Songs (*continued*) 82; "Conquer or Perish" (martial ballad or chorus), 110; "Constitution Glee, The," 67, 72; "Cosmetic Doctor, The," 83, 93, 111; "Country Club," 28, 71
Comic song, 38, 64, 72, 82, 83, 87, 102, 103, 111, 115, 116
"Dan the Waiter's Journey to London," 102; "Day of Marriage, The," 45, 46, 54; "Doctor's Lament, The," 64; "Dr. Splash's Rambles," 72; "Down in the Valley," 91; "Drimindoo," 93, 103
Dirge, in *Romeo and Juliet*, 64, 72, 83, 92, 102; in *The Surrender of Calais*, 111
Duet, 82, 95
Epilogue, to *The Irish Widow*, 64; to *The Jew*, 59; to *John Bull*, 64, 71
Epithalamium, 83, 93
"Fairy of the Glassy Lake," 108; "Faithless Emma," 99, 103; favorite song, 83; "Female Auctioneer, The," 72; "Feyther and I," 71, 72, 111; "Fill the Bowl with Rosy Wine," 64; finale and chorus of *The Travellers,* 94; "Flow Thou Purple Stream," 64; "Flowing Can" (Dibdin), 82; "Four and Twenty Fiddlers," 60; "Frolicsome Fellow," 28
"Galley Slave, The," 83; "Gentle Cousin John," 83; "Gentle Cousin Julia," 102; "Get Away Sorrow," 102; "Ghost" song, 93; "Giles Scroggins' Ghost," 87, 89, 92, 99, 103, 111, 116; "Giordanis," 22; "Girl of My Heart," 102; "Glasses Sparkle on the Board, The," 99; "Glee," 54; "Glorious Apollo," (glee), 92; "Go to the Devil and Shake Yourself," 102; "Grizzle and Pigs," 87;

"Group of Lovers or Beauty at Her Levee, The," 54
"Hard Times or Always A-grumbling," 116; "Hark Hark from the Woodlands," 27; "Here's a Health to all Good Lasses," 64, 71, 72, 92 (glee), 99; "Here's a Nice New Bow-Wow," 28; "Her Mouth with a Smile," 60; "He Stole My Heart Away," 87; "Hobbies, The," 29, 102; "Host That Fought for Liberty, The," 98; "How to Nail 'em," 116; hunting song, 54, 64
"Irish Haymaker, The," 72; "I Say, My Hearts, Why There's Your Work," 69
"Jubilee Song, The," 70, 99; "Just Like Love," 82, 93
"Kate Karney," 93; "Knowing Joe," 83, 93, 94, 103, 111, 116
"Last Night I Sate Me Down and Cried," 109; "Last Week I Took a Wife," 109; "Learned Pig, The," 64; "Let Us All Be Unhappy Together," 111; "Like the Wind Driven Snow" (chorus), 109; "Little Jane of the Mill," 115; "Little Sailor Boy," 27; "Lord Mayor's Show, The," 93; "Love Letter, The," 92; "Lucy," 33; "Lurk, Lurk O'er the Green Sward, 93
"Madam Fig's Gala," 93, 103, 111; "Mad Bess" (cantata, words by Milton, music by Purcell), 33, 54; "Maid of Lodi, The," 93, 103; "Man of All Trades, The," 102; "Marriage is a Lottery," 68, 72; "Masquerade Song, The," 71; "Master Jackey Gilpin's Intended Journey to Brighton," 111; "Mid-Watch, The," 33, 53; "Miss Deborah Diddle," 111; "Mounseer

Songs (continued)
Nong-Tong-Paw," 28, 29; "Mrs. Bond," 93; "Mulberry Tree, The," 70, 99; "Murder in Irish," 83; "My Fine Shepherds of Late" (Arne), 47; "My Mother Had a Maid Called Barbara," 92; "My Sweet Molly Mog," 93 "Nature Will Prevail or a Woman," 72; "Negro Philosophy," 28; "New Quack, The," 28; "Nobody Coming to Bury Me," 116; "Nobody Coming to Marry Me," 116; "Nosegay Girl, The," 46; "Now's the Time for Mirth and Glee," 28 "Ode, The Masonic," 54 "O Fair Lady," 71, 72; "Oh Lady Fair" (Moore), 82; "Oh What a Charming Thing's a Battle," 33; "Old Thomas Day," 102; "Old Woman of Eighty, The," 38, 45; "Owen," 45 "Ploughboy, The," 83; "Poll Primrose," 54; "Poor Thomas Day," 72; "Post Captain, The," 53, 60; "Professional Grinders," 28; "Pronounce the charm and split the rock" (chant), 109 "Red Cross Knights, The," 72, 83, 92; "Rose, The," 92; roundelay and chorus, 37, 99 "Sailor Boy, The," 27; "Sailor's Journal, The," 28; "Sandy O'er the Lee," 116; "Sea Storm, The," (Stevens), 22; "See That Pretty Creature There," 82; "Sigh No More, Ladies," 64, 72, 92, 99; "Sir Gilbert-Go-Softly of Gooseberry Hill," 111; "Soldier is the Noblest Name, A," 87; "Soldier Tired of War's Alarms, The," 49, 64, 82, 86; "Standard of Freedom, The," 98, 99, 103, 111; "Star Spangled Banner, The," 88; "Storm, The," 93; "Strike Minstrels Strike," 110; "Strike the World with Fear and Wonder" (chorus), 109; "Sweet Bird," 116; "Sweet Lillies and Roses," 103; "Sweet Poll of Plymouth," 22; "Sweet Willy O," 70, 99 Songs, 53, 54, 83, 98; by Reinagle, 102, 103, 112, 116; "Masonic," 53; "new patriotic song in praise of the gallant Commodore Preble and his brave tars," 67 "Tars of Columbia, The," 67; "Tell Her I Love Her," 92; "Thorn, The," 92, 93; "Thou Like the Glorious Sun," 33; "Thus For Men and Women Fare," 82; "Tid-Re-I," 68, 72, 83, 93; "Tink-a-Tink" (dancing duet), 83; " 'Tis Liberty, Dear Liberty," (Handel), 47; "To a Woodman's Hut There Came One Day," 109; "Tom Tackle" (Dibdin), 54; "Town Crier, The," 64; "True Glory," 28; trumpet song, 93; "Turn Minutes to Seconds," 103; "Turbanned Turk, The," 60; "Twas You Sir" (catch), 64, 99; "Twiggle and a Friz," 27, 103; "Twins of Latona, The," 33, 103, 116 "Waggoner, The" (Dibdin), 116; "Wander No More My Love," 103; war song, 105; "Warwickshire Thief, The," 70, 99; "What a Woman Is Like," 69; "When Arthur First at Court Began," (glee), 93; "When O'er the Sunshine Clouds Are Cast," 109; "When Sappho Tuned," 82; "While Poor the Spirit Flags," 109; "William Tell," 83; "Within These Shady Bowers," 82; "World's a Good Thing, The," (C. Dib-

Index

Songs (*continued*)
    din), 116; "Wounded Huzzar, The," 60, 64
    "Yorkshire Irishman, The," 86, 93, 111
Son-in-Law, The, 92
Sons of Apollo, The, 91, 92
South Street ("contingent"), 49, 66
South Street Theatre, 26, 51, 59, 60, 61, 67
Southwark (South Street Theatre,) 17, 18, 20, 28, 29, 70, 80, 95, 101, 102, 104, 107
Spanish Barber, The, 41, 45
Speed the Plough, 30, 34, 42, 44, 54, 65, 92, 94, 103, 111
Spence, 82
Spirit of Independence, The, 97, 111
Spoiled Child, The, 22, 71, 78, 116
Stanley, Mrs., 107, 112
Stewart, 17
Story, 70
Stranger, The, 17
Stuart, 23, 100
Such Things Are, 55
Sultan, The, 73
Summers, 89
Surrender of Calais, The, 111
Swan, 26, 27, 51, 60

Tale of Mystery, A, 61, 65, 73, 104
Tale of Terror, A, 62
Tancred and Sigismunda, 95
Taylor, 71, 77, 83, 99
Taylor, Raynor, 119
Tears and Smiles, 91
Tekeli, 110
Tempest, The, 53
Temple of Flora, The, 71
Theatrical Censor, The, 75, 76, 77, 78, 79, 80, 81, 84, 85, 94
Theatrical Censor, The, and Critical Miscellany, 90, 91, 101
"*Theatric Lounge, A,*" 59
Thespian Mirror, The, 113
"Thespian Panorama, The," 26
Thespian Society, 26, 29
Three-Fingered Jack (*Obi or* —), 81
Three Weeks after Marriage, 44

Time's a Tell-tale, 103, 104
To Marry or Not to Marry, 100
Tom Thumb the Great, 99
Touchstone of Truth, The, 29
Toussaint L'Ouverture, 55
Town and Country, 97, 100, 101, 103, 116
Travellers, The, 94
Tripoli, 67, 89
Tripoli (ship), 49
Tripolitan Prize, The, 56, 65
Tripolitans, 68, 69
Trip to Fontainbleau, A, 39, 42
Truxton, 17
Turnbull, 38
Twaits, 57, 63, 64, 68, 69, 71, 72
Two Misers, The, 94
Two Per Cent, 65

University of Pennsylvania, 85
Usher, 34, 38

Valentine and Orson, 90
Vanice, Miss, 26
Venice Preserved, 20, 21, 29, 34, 52, 53, 102, 104
Vintner in the Suds, 27
Virginia (natural bridge in), 69
Virgin of the Son, The, 53
Virginia theatre, 86
Voice of Nature, The, 84
Votary of Wealth, The, 30

Wadsworth, 89
Walnut Street Theatre, 32, 107
Warrell, 72
Warrell (Junior), 22
Warren, 16, 41, 42, 43, 48, 52, 54, 59, 65, 70, 76, 80, 85, 88, 90, 91, 97, 105, 107, 111, 113, 118
Warren, Mrs. (formerly Mrs. Merry, Mrs. Wignell), 64, 90, 92, 102, 103, 105, 107, 119
Warren, General, 38, 110
Washington (city), 29, 34, 84
Washington, George, 23; "apotheosis of," 17; as "first in war," etc., 115; at levee, 16; cantering with his officers, 16; death, 15, 20; honor of birthday, 88; Monody on, 28; support of theatre, 52, 118

Washington, Martha, 48
Ways and Means, 108
Way to Get Married, The, 55, 69, 83, 93
Way to Keep Him, The, 38
Weathercock, The, 90, 116
Webster, 87, 91, 92, 93, 95, 97, 98, 99, 102, 103
Wedding in Wales, A, 43, 44, 46
West (actor), 116
West, Benjamin, 20
West Indian, The, 77, 80, 114
Westray, Ellen (later Mrs. J. Darley), 33
Westray, Juliana (later Mrs. Wood), 33, 42, 43, 50, 64
Whale, Master, 38
What Would the Man Be At?, 44
Wheel of Fortune, The, 117
Wheel of Truth, The, 65
Which Is the Man?, 54, 111
Whitlock, 52
Whitlock, Mrs., 40, 41, 42, 43, 44, 52
Who Pays the Piper?, 111
Who Wants a Guinea?, 78
Widow of Malabar, The, 45
Wife of Two Husbands, The, 71
Wignell, 16, 17, 18, 20, 24, 29, 30, 34, 36, 41, 42, 44, 46, 50, 52, 55, 113, 118
Wignell, Mrs. (formerly Mrs. Merry), 52, 59, 78, 80, 83, 84, 88
Will, The, 33
William Penn or the Landing of our Forefathers, 29
Williams, Mr., 104
Wilmot, 101, 102
Wilmot, Mrs. (formerly Mrs. Marshall), 101, 102, 104, 112, 115, 116
Wilson, 37
Windsor Wags, 43, 45
Wonder, The, 107, 112
Wood, 39, 41, 42, 43, 48, 50, 52, 57, 58, 59, 67, 76, 77, 79, 80, 84, 85, 88, 90, 91, 97, 101, 105, 107, 111, 118
Wood, Mrs. (formerly Juliana Westray), 77
Wood Daemon, The, 110
Woodham, 75, 78, 79, 80, 82, 83, 92, 93, 95, 107
Woodham, Mrs., 80, 82, 83, 84, 89, 91, 92, 94
Workman, James, 66
Wounded Huzzar, The, 110
Wreath for American Tars, A, or Huzza Again for the Constitution, 17

Yellow fever, 18, 24, 30, 49, 50, 55, 73
Youth, Love and Folly, 103